Green Marketing
in a Unified Europe

Green Marketing in a Unified Europe

Alma Mintu-Wimsatt, PhD
Héctor R. Lozada, PhD
Editors

Routledge
Taylor & Francis Group

LONDON AND NEW YORK

First published 1996 by International Business Press

2 Park Square, Milton Park, Abingdon, Oxon OX14 4RN
711 Third Avenue, New York, NY 10017, USA

Routledge is an imprint of the Taylor & Francis Group, an informa business

First issued in paperback 2016

Transferred to Digital Printing 2010 by Routledge

Green Marketing in a Unified Europe has also been published as *Journal of Euromarketing*, Volume 5, Number 3 1996.

Library of Congress Cataloging-in-Publication Data

Green marketing in a unified Europe/ Alma Mintu-Wimsatt, Héctor R. Lozada, editors.
    p. cm.
    "Has also been published as Journal of Euromarketing, Vol. 5, number 3, 1996"– verso t.p.
    Includes bibliographical references and index.
    ISBN 1-56024-829-7 (alk. paper)
    1. Green marketing–Europe. I. Mintu-Wimsatt, Alma T. II. Lozada, Héctor R. III. Journal of Euromarketing.
HF5413.G726 1996   96-27827
658.8–dc20   CIP

ISBN 978-1-56024-829-3 (hbk)
ISBN 978-1-138-99206-1 (pbk)

INDEXING & ABSTRACTING

Contributions to this publication are selectively indexed or abstracted in print, electronic, online, or CD-ROM version(s) of the reference tools and information services listed below. This list is current as of the copyright date of this publication. See the end of this section for additional notes.

- *ABI/INFORM Global* (broad-coverage indexing & abstracting service that includes numerous English-language titles outside the USA available from University Microfilms International (UMI), 300 North Zeeb Road, P.O. Box 1346, Ann Arbor, MI 48106-1346), UMI Data Courier, Attn: Library Services, Box 34660, Louisville, KY 40232

- *ABSCAN, Inc.*, P.O. Box 2384, Monroe, LA 71207-2384

- *American Bibliography of Slavic and East European Studies (ABSEES)*, Compiled at the University of Illinois at Urbana-Champaign (246A Library, 1408 W. Gregory Dr., Urbana, IL 61820) under the auspices of the American Asssociation for the Advancement of Slavic Studies (Jordan Quad/Acacia Building, 125 Panama Street, Stanford, CA 94305-4130). Printed editions are published on an annual basis. Citations are also available in ABSEES Online, which can be accessed via the Internet (telnet to alexia.lis.uiuc.edu), or via dial-up connections (217-244-6451). At the "login:" prompt, type "absees"; at the "Password:" prompt, type "slavibib," University of Illinois @ Urbana-Champaign, 246A Library, 1408 West Gregory Drive, Urbana, IL 61801

- *c/o CAB International/CAB ACCESS* . . . available in print, diskettes updated weekly, and on INTERNET. Providing full bibliographic listings, author affiliation, augmented keyword searching, CAB International, P.O. Box 100, Wallingford Oxon OX10 8DE, United Kingdom

- *Cabell's Directory of Publishing Opportunities in Business & Economics* (comprehensive & descriptive bibliographic listing with editorial criteria and publication production data for selected business & economics journals), Cabell Publishing Company, Box 5428, Tobe Hahn Station, Beaumont, TX 77726-5428

- *CNPIEC Reference Guide: Chinese National Directory of Foreign Periodicals*, P.O. Box 88, Beijing, Peoples Republic of China

- *Contents Pages in Management*, University of Manchester Business School, Booth Street West, Manchester M15 6PB, England

(continued)

- **Foods Adlibra**, Foods Adlibra Publications, 9000 Plymouth Avenue North, Minneapolis, MN 55427

- **GEO Abstracts (GEO Abstracts/GEOBASE),** Elsevier/GEO Abstracts, Regency House, 34 Duke Street, Norwich NR3 3AP, England

- **Human Resources Abstracts (HRA)**, Sage Publications, Inc., 2455 Teller Road, Newbury Park, CA 91320

- **INTERNET ACCESS (& additional networks) Bulletin Board for Libraries ("BUBL"), coverage of information resources on INTERNET, JANET, and other networks.**
  - JANET X.29: UK.AC.BATH.BUBL or 00006012101300
  - TELNET: BUBL.BATH.AC.UK or 138.38.32.45 login 'bubl'
  - Gopher: BUBL.BATH.AC.UK (138.32.32.45). Port 7070
  - World Wide Web: http: / / www.bubl.bath.ac.uk./BUBL/ home.html
  - NISSWAIS: telnetniss.ac. uk (for the NISS gateway)
  The Andersonian Library, Curran Building, 101 St. James Road, Glasgow G4 ONS, Scotland

- **Journal of Health Care Marketing (abstracts section)**, Georgia Tech-School of Management, Ivan Allen College, 225 North Avenue NW, Atlanta, GA 30332

- **Management & Marketing Abstracts**, Pira International, Randalls Road, Leatherhead, Surrey KT22 7RU, England

- **Market Research Abstracts,** The Market Research Society, 17 Kenelm Close, Harrow HA1 3TE, England

- **Operations Research/Management Science**, Executive Sciences Institute, 1005 Mississippi Avenue, Davenport, IA 52803

- **Sage Public Administration Abstracts (SPAA)**, Sage Publications, Inc., 2455 Teller Road, Newbury Park, CA 91320

- **Sage Urban Studies Abstracts (SUSA)**, Sage Publications, Inc., 2455 Teller Road, Newbury Park, CA 91320

- **Social Planning/Policy & Development Abstracts (SOPODA)**, Sociological Abstracts, Inc., P.O. Box 22206, San Diego, CA 92192-0206

- **Sociological Abstracts (SA)**, Sociological Abstracts, Inc., P.O. Box 22206, San Diego, CA 92192-0206

- **World Agricultural Economics & Rural Sociology Abstracts,** CAB Abstracts, CAB International, Wallingford Oxon OX10 8DE, England

(continued)

SPECIAL BIBLIOGRAPHIC NOTES

related to special journal issues (separates)
and indexing/abstracting

☐ indexing/abstracting services in this list will also cover material in any "separate" that is co-published simultaneously with Haworth's special thematic journal issue or DocuSerial. Indexing/abstracting usually covers material at the article/chapter level.

☐ monographic co-editions are intended for either non-subscribers or libraries which intend to purchase a second copy for their circulating collections.

☐ monographic co-editions are reported to all jobbers/wholesalers/approval plans. The source journal is listed as the "series" to assist the prevention of duplicate purchasing in the same manner utilized for books-in-series.

☐ to facilitate user/access services all indexing/abstracting services are encouraged to utilize the co-indexing entry note indicated at the bottom of the first page of each article/chapter/contribution.

☐ this is intended to assist a library user of any reference tool (whether print, electronic, online, or CD-ROM) to locate the monographic version if the library has purchased this version but not a subscription to the source journal.

☐ individual articles/chapters in any Haworth publication are also available through the Haworth Document Delivery Services (HDDS).

Green Marketing in a Unified Europe

CONTENTS

ABOUT THE EDITORS

Alma Mintu-Wimsatt (PhD, University of Kentucky) is Associate Professor, Department of Marketing & Management, East Texas State University. Her research interests include international negotiations and green marketing. She has published in *Management Science, European Journal of Marketing, Journal of Global Business, Marketing Education Review, Journal of Marketing Theory & Practice,* and *Journal of Teaching in International Business.*

Héctor R. Lozada (PhD, University of Kentucky) is Visiting Assistant Professor, Department of Marketing/Faculty of Management, Rutgers University-Newark. His research interests include marketing strategy and product planning, interpretive approaches to marketing and consumer research, and green marketing. He has published in *Journal of Consumer Research, Journal of Organizational Change Management, Marketing Education Review, Journal of Business & Industrial Marketing,* and *Journal of Teaching in International Business.*

Preface

I am very pleased to be able to present a special volume on *Green Marketing in a Unified Europe*. This is a very important area of marketing where there is very little internationally based information and research material. Professors Alma Mintu-Wimsatt and Héctor R. Lozada are to be congratulated for bringing this special collection together. My sincere hope is that we may conduct more research at cross-cultural, cross-national and comparative levels. Green marketing is not only a concern of developed countries of the North, but we also need understanding of green marketing issues pertaining to developing countries of the South.

The phrase or term green marketing has become an important buzzword for research and marketing practise in the 1990s. Many company managers in different parts of the world claim that in order to be competitive and distinguish themselves in the marketplace, the preservation, protection, and conservation of the physical and ecological environment have to be integrated as part of a company's strategic agenda and this has got to be an important part of its strategic planning process. As such, this book explores some of the facets by which green marketing has been effectively integrated in the practice of international marketing.

From a macro perspective, Vastag, Rondinelli and Kerekes investigate the perceptions Hungarian managers have of environmental challenges. They discovered that Hungarian managers' perceptions did not significantly differ from those of their

[Haworth co-indexing entry note]: "Preface." Kaynak, Erdener. Co-published simultaneously in *Journal of Euromarketing* (International Business Press, an imprint of The Haworth Press, Inc.) Vol. 5, No. 3, 1996, pp. xiii-xv; and: *Green Marketing in a Unified Europe* (ed: Alma Mintu-Wimsatt, and Héctor R. Lozada) International Business Press, an imprint of The Haworth Press, Inc., 1996, pp. xi-xiii. Single or multiple copies of this article are available from The Haworth Document Delivery Service [1-800-342-9678, 9:00 a.m. - 5:00 p.m. (EST). E-mail address: getinfo@haworth.com].

Western European and North American counterparts. That is, survey results suggest that Hungarian managers are well aware of today's environmental plight and that companies will have to invest more in order to achieve higher levels of environmental protection.

From a micro perspective, Whitson and Henry look at the green labeling practices of marketers. While it appears that many consumers are unclear about the "greenness" terminology in labels, there is some evidence that these consumers place value on companies' outward display of environmental responsibility.

The paper by Titterington et al. reviews previous market research into consumer behaviour in the United Kingdom and elsewhere. In particular it looks at the various classifications of green consumerism that have been put forward. It presents a summary of the results of a series of longitudinal studies of the purchase of environmentally friendly products and other "green" activity by Northern Ireland consumers. From these studies the breadth and depth of commitment of the green consumer is identified and combined to provide an overall classification of green consumerism in Northern Ireland.

The results of the various studies carried out in Northern Ireland, when compared to the results of studies carried out in the rest of the United Kingdom, exhibit striking similarities, leading us to conclude that the Northern Ireland consumer exhibits similar environmental concern, commitment and behaviour to their fellow citizens on the mainland. As such, this would tend to indicate that many of the findings from the UK research are applicable to Northern Ireland and vice versa. It also highlights the fact that Northern Ireland manufacturers need to take due cognisance of the fact that they, to some degree, lag behind UK manufacturers in evolving strategies to meet some of the threats and take full advantage of the opportunities posed by green consumerism.

With environmental concern receiving massive media attention globally, it is no surprise that environmentalism was forced near the top of political agendas throughout the world and certainly on government and opposition parties' agendas in the UK. This political promotion of environmental issues plus the continuing media focus helped stimulate mainstream public concern about environmental problems.

Finally, Editors Lozada and Mintu-Wimsatt provide a green marketing framework based on past literature with the introduction of the concept called "sustainable development." Sustainable development encourages voluntary responses from various constituent groups that have contributed to the deterioration of the natural environment.

There is much to be done in this fertile and under-researched area of marketing. Unfortunately, much more is said than done as far as green marketing is concerned in North America, despite all of the talk and debates within the framework of NAFTA and bilateral negotiations between U.S.A. and Canada. Our European counterparts and even Japan are far ahead of North American countries. For effective green marketing policies, rules and regulations we need a good research base which, I think, is sorely missing at this stage of development of our discipline. I wholeheartedly encourage our contributors and readers to pay more attention to the subject matter of green marketing in the future.

Erdener Kaynak

Introduction

Alma Mintu-Wimsatt
Héctor R. Lozada

> Environmental protection and sustainable development must be an integral part of the mandates of all agencies of governments, of international organizations, and of major private-sector institutions.
>
> —World Commission on Environment and Development
> *Our Common Future*

Two decades ago, businesses' and society's interests reached an impasse. At the center of the debate was the philosophy of *limits to growth*, which promoted the idea that both population and economic growth should be limited in favor of an alternative low-technology lifestyle in symbiosis with nature (Pearce, 1991). The main thrust of this philosophy was the belief that legislation alone could help protect, preserve, and conserve our physical environment. Consequently, in November 1973, the European Community (presently known as the European Union) adopted the First Action Programme on the Environment (Pearce, 1991). This program, and the three others that followed, endorsed a comprehensive approach and sought to tackle water and air pollution problems, improve the management of wastes, and protect wildlife and habitats. About 200 pieces of legislation resulted from these four action plans.

Alma Mintu-Wimsatt is affiliated with East Texas State University and Héctor R. Lozada is affiliated with Binghamton University (SUNY).

[Haworth co-indexing entry note]: "Introduction." Mintu-Wimsatt, Alma, and Héctor R. Lozada. Co-published simultaneously in *Journal of Euromarketing* (International Business Press, an imprint of The Haworth Press, Inc.) Vol. 5, No. 3, 1996, pp. 1-4; and: *Green Marketing in a Unified Europe* (ed: Alma Mintu-Wimsatt, and Héctor R. Lozada) International Business Press, an imprint of The Haworth Press, Inc., 1996, pp. 1-4. Single or multiple copies of this article are available from The Haworth Document Delivery Service [1-800-342-9678, 9:00 a.m. - 5:00 p.m. (EST). E-mail address: getinfo@haworth.com.].

1

Presently, however, the realization that legislation alone is not sufficient to provide solutions to environmental problems seems to dominate the debate. As a result, we have seen in the 1990s a move toward the cessation of confrontational approaches like the ones exemplified by the 1970s. Instead, a different philosophical approach has gained momentum in the latter part of the 20th Century. Sustainable development, as forwarded in the report titled *Our Common Future* (World Commission on Environment and Development, 1987), attempts to promote a balance between human activity and the ability of nature to renew itself. Although controversial, the philosophy of sustainable development favors cooperation, limited legislation, and the encouragement of voluntary responses from all parties involved in the deterioration of our physical environment: businesses, governments, and societies.

In December 1992, the European Union adopted the 5th Environmental Action Programme, which significantly differs from the previous four in its subscription to the goals of sustainability advanced in the 1992 Earth Summit. It is in this context that we envisioned this special collection. With this volume we want to promote the debate on the implications of sustainable development as we approach the new century. The European Union provides an interesting background for these discussions, given the attempts at the promotion of a unified environmental vision, and the individual proclivities of member states to embrace environmental initiatives.

We follow the premise that an important item in the strategic agenda of international marketers is the physical environment and its preservation, protection, and conservation. We believe that opportunities exist for businesses to competitively position themselves through an environment-friendly philosophy, while acting in a socially and environmentally responsible manner. Moreover, we submit that opportunities exist for business organizations to competitively position themselves through a pro-environment stance. To provide a more focused presentation, we decided to frame our discussion within the context of the European Union. Because of this, we (1) invited several distinguished scholars to submit manuscripts relevant to the theme of this book, and (2) relied on an open

Call for Papers to develop a collection of manuscripts. All articles were subjected to the normal double-blind refereeing process.

The collection of articles included in this volume reveals the repercussions that the topic has on the corporate world, on governments and governmental agencies, and on societies. First, Vastag, Rondinelli, and Kerekes present the results of a survey comparing the environmental perceptions of Hungarian managers with those of managers from around the world. Their article offers an interesting contrast in current perceptions, while highlighting the realization of all managers that environmental concerns have strategic dimensions that may be too critical to ignore.

Whitson and Henry's presentation spotlights the issue of "greenness" in products and in labeling practices. Consumers have shown conflicting perceptions and a degree of confusion regarding environmental friendliness of products. Nevertheless, their article underscores the existence of evidence to confirm that certain consumers value the environmental drives of manufacturers.

Titterington, Davies, and Cochrane assess green consumerism in Northern Ireland relative to the United Kingdom. Their investigation suggests similarities in the environmental concern, commitment, and behaviors between these two groups. However, some evidence exists that the UK's manufacturers appear to be ahead in their efforts to take advantage of the business ramifications of the green movement.

To close this collection, we explore the philosophy of sustainable development. Our approach focuses on how the concepts associated with sustainability are affecting environmental policy-making in the European Union, and are, consequently, impacting the practices of companies (particularly multinational ones) doing business in Europe.

We appreciate the encouragement and support that we received from the very beginning from *Journal of Euromarketing* editor, Erdener Kaynak. Additionally, we want to thank Dr. Keith McFarland, Dean of the Graduate School at East Texas State University for his financial support to this project. Finally, we are indebted to the ad hoc reviewers whose prompt responses and constructive comments provided timely and valuable insights. We want to acknowledge their names:

Anthony Di Benedetto – Temple University
John Ford – Old Dominion University
Jule Gassenheimer – University of Kentucky
Robert Hogner – Florida International University
Earl Honeycutt – Old Dominion University
Alfred Lewis – Binghamton University
Lou Pelton – University of North Texas
Mark Young – Winona State University

This volume represents the continuation of research and conversations on green marketing that we have pursued since 1991. It is our hope that this collection of articles provides additional impetus to the interesting debates on green issues that gained momentum in marketing journals and in marketing conferences in the past few years.

REFERENCES

Pearce, D. (1991). Environmentalism and Business. In *The Greening of Business,* Rhys A. David (ed.), Brookfield, VT: Gower Publishing Co., 1-10.
World Commission on Environment and Development (1987). *Our Common Future.* Oxford: Oxford University Press.

How Corporate Executives Perceive Environmental Issues: Comparing Hungarian and Global Companies

Gyula Vastag
Dennis A. Rondinelli
Sándor Kerekes

SUMMARY. This article reports the results of a survey conducted in Hungary to compare the environmental perceptions of Hungarian corporate managers with those of other executives from around the world who had earlier responded to a similar survey conducted by McKinsey and Company. The results showed virtually no differences in how Hungarian managers perceived the importance of environmental challenges, but they did reveal stronger differences in perceptions between Hungarian and international respondents and among Hungarian respondents from companies in different owner-

Gyula Vastag is Senior Research Associate at the Kenan Institute of Private Enterprise, Kenan-Flagler Business School, University of North Carolina, Campus Box 3440, Chapel Hill, NC 27599-3440, USA. Email: VASTAGG.BSACD1 @MHS.UNC.EDU. Dennis A. Rondinelli is Glaxo Distinguished International Professor and Director of the Center for Global Business Research at the Kenan Institute of Private Enterprise, Kenan-Flagler Business School, University of North Carolina. Email: RONDINED.BSACD1@MHS.UNC.EDU. Sándor Kerekes is Professor and Chair, Department of Environmental Economics and Technology, Budapest University of Economic Sciences, Budapest IX, Kinizsi u.1-7, H-1092 Budapest, Hungary. Email: KKTT001@URSUS.BKE.HU.

[Haworth co-indexing entry note]: "How Corporate Executives Perceive Environmental Issues: Comparing Hungarian and Global Companies." Vastag, Gyula, Dennis A. Rondinelli, and Sándor Kerekes. Co-published simultaneously in *Journal of Euromarketing* (International Business Press, an imprint of The Haworth Press, Inc.) Vol. 5, No. 3, 1996, pp. 5-27; and: *Green Marketing in a Unified Europe* (ed: Alma Mintu-Wimsatt, and Héctor R. Lozada) International Business Press, an imprint of The Haworth Press, Inc., 1996, pp. 5-27. Single or multiple copies of this article are available from The Haworth Document Delivery Service [1-800-342-9678, 9:00 a.m. - 5:00 p.m. (EST). E-mail address: getinfo@haworth.com.].

ship groups on how companies were putting their environmental concerns into practice. Although there seems to be a wider gap between executives of Hungarian companies and those from Western Europe and North America in adopting environmental practices, the survey revealed that Hungarian managers are acutely aware that their companies will have to invest more heavily to achieve higher levels of environmental protection in the future. *[Article copies available from The Haworth Document Delivery Service: 1-800-342-9678. E-mail address: getinfo@haworth.com].*

INTRODUCTION

Executives in Central Europe must operate in complex and uncertain economic conditions as their countries undergo a transition from socialist to market systems. The transition affects every segment of society (Jackson et al., 1993). One of the most critical challenges facing Hungarian managers is how to resolve the conflicting pressures of attaining financial stability for their companies while at the same time coping with potentially serious problems such as environmental pollution. The stereotype of managers from third world or formerly communist countries as being oblivious to or unconcerned about the dangers of environmental degradation arises from the belief that the government and the private sector continue to avoid the costs of environmental protection and cleanup (Pearson, 1987). Although Hungary's economy is just emerging from a long period of stagnation and its GDP per capita ranks only 56 among the 160 countries for which the World Bank and the United Nations Development Program provide comparative economic statistics, its human development index (the combination of GDP per capita, illiteracy rate, average number of years spent in school and life expectancy) ranks higher than some Western European countries (World Bank, 1994). Because education levels and environmental awareness are correlated, the concern for a clean environment should be relatively high in a country like Hungary. Given Hungary's human development index and its desire to become a member of the European Economic Community, its corporate executives should be willing to adopt higher environmental standards as quickly as possible.

Although many Hungarian managers may still consider the costs of meeting environmental challenges a threat to their companies' competitiveness, the growing pressures from nongovernment organizations and consumers for environmentally sound production processes and environmentally-friendly products are likely to push them more quickly toward meeting global market requirements (Cairncross, 1992; Schmidheiny, 1992). Moreover, government officials and business leaders in Central Europe are coming to realize that stricter environmental regulations and stronger enforcement can protect the region from the transfer of obsolete and highly polluting production technologies (Frosch & Gallopulas, 1989; Kemp, 1993).

Pressures on Hungarian companies interested in attracting foreign investment also arise from the fact that over the past few years multinational corporations have become increasingly sensitive to the environmental impacts of their business practices and operations (Schot & Fischer, 1993). An increasing number of companies recognize that in the global marketplace, their environmental image affects the demand for their products, their ability to obtain loans from international financial institutions, and the sale of their shares on international stock exchanges (UNCTC, 1990). Even in formerly socialist countries and in developing economies where governments and the private sector paid little attention to the environmental consequences of industrial activity during the past half century, governments are increasingly being pressured by international organizations and local interest groups to adopt stronger environmental regulations and to encourage companies to use "green" business practices (Panayotou, 1993).

Although there seems to be a growing consensus among corporate executives in multinational companies that they must take environmental impacts into account, little is known about how extensively such perceptions are shared by companies that are not owned by or that do not generally trade with multinational firms, or about how the perceptions of environmental issues are translated into business policy and operations within manufacturing firms in emerging market countries. Many questions remain about the significance of environmental issues in business practice. Do multinational companies operate differently in countries such as Hungary that less stringently enforce environmental regulations than they do in countries with stronger environmental laws and enforcement? Do widespread perceptions of the need for companies to be sensitive to the environmental impacts of their operations extend deeply into firms in formerly communist countries in Central and Eastern Europe, where environmental problems are severe and the environmental impacts of their operations were largely ignored for more than 40 years? Do managers of multinational companies in Central and Eastern European countries such as Hungary perceive any differently the need to improve environmental conditions than managers of their parent companies in Western Europe or North America?

This article explores answers to some of these questions by examining the perceptions of corporate executives throughout the world of the importance of environmental protection to their business strategies and operations; by comparing international perceptions with those of executives in one country, Hungary, that is in transition from a socialist to a market-oriented economy and that suffers from serious environmental problems; and by comparing the environmental perceptions of executives of companies within Hungary under different forms of ownership. The impact of ownership on the way in which executives and managers perceive environmental issues has received little attention in the literature.

ENVIRONMENTAL PROBLEMS AND ECONOMIC CONDITIONS IN HUNGARY

The challenges facing multinational and local companies around the world in dealing with environmental issues are no more critical than in the former socialist countries of Central and Eastern Europe (Vári & Tamás, 1993). Since 1989 the economic situation and the political map of Central Europe have changed dramatically, and the implications of these changes will be critical for multinational companies seeking to invest in or export to the region. Among the new democracies of this region, Hungary, Poland, and the Czech Republic have the best chance to become an integral part of the European Community, but to do so they must address their environmental problems and pursue higher environmental standards.

Although Central European countries have made relatively good progress toward economic reform and the restructuring of the ownership of their industries since 1990, they face two critical challenges in the decade ahead. First, they must restructure their domestic industries and attract investment by multinational companies (MNCs) in order to become competitive in world markets (Rondinelli, 1993). The ongoing privatization and the growing number of joint ventures in Hungary, for example, are already changing the way many companies are managing their internal functions, including manufacturing (Rondinelli & Fellenz, 1993). But more profound and widespread changes will have to occur in the future in order for Central European countries such as Hungary to meet the stricter standards of quality, flexibility, delivery time, and service required by global markets. Second, both domestic and multinational manufacturing companies in Hungary and in other Central European countries will have to adjust to growing demands by both local residents and international organizations for environmental protection and clean-up (Hansen, 1989). Traditionally, environmental issues played a minor role in decisions of companies in centrally planned economies. Because they were state-owned enterprises against which environmental regulations were not stringently enforced by the government, manufacturing and mining industries in Hungary, for example, could largely ignore the environmental impacts of their operations under the socialist regime. Now, with the adoption of stricter environmental regulations and the growing demand for environmental cleanup there is a chance that this situation will change, and industrial enterprises will have to modify their manufacturing processes accordingly. Although Hungary has environmental protection laws and regulations, they have only been casually enforced since the demise of the communist regime. The desire of Hungary to join the European Economic Community and the pressures of international financing organizations such as the World Bank and the European Bank for Reconstruction and Development on the Hungarian government to clean up environmental pollution and enact and enforce more stringent regulations will increase the pressures on businesses to address environmental management issues.

New legislation on environmental protection is being considered by the Hungarian Parliament along with new regulations that require environmental impact assessments for a wide range of industries, new land use and construction regulations, and new legislation on handling, storage, and disposal of chemical hazardous materials. In the early 1990s Hungary upgraded regulatory standards for air quality and defined more clearly monitoring and control requirements, placed limits on vehicular air emissions, and increased fines for polluting rivers, lakes and groundwater. Since the late 1980s, the Hungarian government has also signed international conventions on environmental impact assessment, control of transboundary movements of hazardous wastes and their disposal, and long-range transboundary air pollution, and signed the Montreal Protocol on Substances that Deplete the Ozone Layer (White & Case, Inc., 1994). If the new legislation and agreements are enforced, those industries that have the highest potential for polluting air and water resources will have to find ways of building environmental restrictions and targets into their manufacturing processes.

COMPARING ENVIRONMENTAL PERCEPTIONS INTERNATIONALLY AND IN HUNGARY

The purpose of this article is to assess the perceptions of environmental challenges and practices among executives of manufacturing firms in three ownership groups in Hungary and to compare them with perceptions of corporate executives in other parts of the world. A questionnaire for Hungarian corporate executives was developed to compare their responses with those of executives who participated in a worldwide survey conducted by McKinsey and Company in 1991 (McKinsey & Company, 1991).

The McKinsey study elicited responses from corporate executives who attended three international conferences and from targeted groups to ensure sufficient responses from developing countries in Latin America, Southeast Asia, and other regions (26% of respondents) and from Central and Eastern Europe (12%) in addition to those received from executives from Western Europe (34%), North America (17%) and Japan (11%). The five regions were based on the geographic location and the GNP per capita of the country where the company's headquarters were located. McKinsey sent out about 1,400 questionnaires, and received a total of 447 completed forms, a 30% response.[1]

The Hungarian survey was carried out about a year after the McKinsey international survey. Many of the same questions were translated from English to Hungarian and some new questions about company ownership were added. The translation was made by a Hungarian doctoral candidate at the Budapest University of Economic Sciences and verified by one of the authors. Question-naires were sent to 400 medium- or large-sized companies that were on the membership list of the Hungarian Chamber of Commerce. The 42% response rate in Hungary–169 company executives–was itself an indicator of the strong interest in this topic. However, as is quite common in surveys, not all of the respondents answered all of the questions and, thus, the actual number of respondents varies from question to question.

CHARACTERISTICS OF THE HUNGARIAN SAMPLE

As in the McKinsey survey, the respondents to the Hungarian questionnaires were mostly senior managers, including managing directors, CEOs, and corporate department heads. The McKinsey international responses were largely from executives in companies in the chemicals, energy, metals, processing, consumer goods and durables industries.[2] The international survey did not identify re-spondents by their companies' ownership characteristics. In the Hungarian sample, shown in Table 1, companies were divided into three ownership groups based on the assumption that foreign own-ership probably has some influence on the management style of the company. This differentiation makes it possible to verify whether or not foreign investment is dominant in highly polluting industries.

The majority of the companies–125 establishments–were domes-tic Hungarian companies and were fully owned by Hungarian insti-tutions. The second group, 30 companies, represented mixed own-ership. In this group the average foreign ownership was 52%. The third group consisted of six companies fully owned by foreign investors. Those companies that did not give information about their ownership were not included in this analysis.

Table 2 lists the industries included in the survey. Table 3 shows that most of the companies in all ownership groups were involved in manufacturing, although a few were engaged in assembling, trading, forwarding or warehousing. Table 4 indicates the size categories of companies by number of employees.

Domestic Companies. The largest subsample of executives was from domestically-owned companies (78.7% of all companies in the sample), including light industries such as wood processing, paper, and textiles. Executives from companies in the chemical industry (e.g., pharmaceutical, rubber, and cosmetics) and the food industry made up 17.2 and 16.4% respectively of the sample. Respondents from machine factories represented 12.9% in this ownership category. Hardly any foreign investment was found in the chemical industry because Hungary's environmental liability regu-

TABLE 1. Legal Structures by Ownership Types

Legal Type	Ownership		
	Domestic	Mixed	Foreign
Limited liability company	29 (23.2%)	11 (36.7%)	5 (83.3%)
Joint stock company	52 (41.6%)	19 (63.3%)	1 (16.7%)
Cooperative	5 (4.0%)	0 (0%)	0 (0%)
State owned company	34 (27.2%)	0 (0%)	0 (0%)
No answer	5 (4.0%)	0 (0%)	0 (0%)
Total	125 (100.0%)	30 (100.0%)	6 (100.0%)

TABLE 2. Industries of Companies Surveyed

Industry	Domestic	Mixed	Foreign
Mining	1	1	0
Electric Energy Production	2	0	0
Metallurgy	7	0	0
Machine Factory	15	3	0
Construction Materials	1	3	2
Chemicals	20	2	0
Light Industries	30	3	0
Food Industry	20	9	2
Transportation	4	1	0
Trade	7	3	1
Other	11	3	1

TABLE 3. Activities of Companies

Type of Activity	Domestic	Mixed	Foreign
Mining	1	0	0
Manufacturing	84	22	5
Assembling	8	2	0
Trade	8	3	1
Forwarding, Warehousing	1	2	0
Construction	1	0	0
Other	20	1	0

TABLE 4. Number of Employees by Ownership
(Percentage Distribution)

Number of Employees	Domestic	Mixed	Foreign
Fewer than 50	9.8	16.7	16.7
Between 50 and 250	26.0	20.0	50.0
Between 250 and 500	17.9	10.0	0.0
More than 500	46.3	53.3	33.3
Total	100.0	100.0	100.0

lations make new owners of privatized companies fully liable for clean-up of the site. Many of the domestic companies were still either state-owned enterprises (27%) or joint stock companies in which the government may still own a portion of the shares (41.6%). About 46% of these enterprises were large, with more than 500 employees, and about 64% had more than 250 employees.

Mixed-Ownership Companies. Respondents from most companies with mixed ownership were in the food industry. The other sectors—machine factories, construction materials, light industries, and trade—were about equally represented by about 10.7% of the respondents. A majority of these enterprises were joint stock companies. More than 53% of these mixed-ownership companies had more than 500 employees. Only about 17% were small companies with less than 50 workers.

Foreign-Owned Companies. Two of the six foreign-owned companies produced construction materials, two others were in the food industry, and the remaining two were engaged in trade. As might be expected, five of the six wholly foreign-owned companies were limited liability corporations and one was a joint stock company. Two of the companies had more than 500 employees; the other four had fewer than 250 workers.

Perceptions of Environmental Issues

Both the McKinsey international survey and the Hungarian corporate survey sought to understand how strongly corporate executives recognized environmental issues and their perceptions of how government and the business community can begin to deal with them. In both questionnaires, executives were asked about their reactions to seven statements and to indicate on a five-point scale (1 = fully disagree, 5 = fully agree) the extent to which they agreed with these statements. The results show a high level of recognition of how serious environmental problems are in countries around the world. The Hungarian responses also allowed differences between perceptions of executives in companies in different ownership groups to be tested. The Kruskal-Wallis non-parametric test was used to indicate differences among the ownership groups in Hungary. This powerful test is the nonparametric equivalent of the analysis of variance and it is more appropriate for the analysis of data with potential outliers (Daniel, 1990). Table 5 shows the statements posed to corporate executives in both surveys and the significance level of the test for the Hungarian group where significant differences appeared. In order to make the Hungarian study comparable with the McKinsey survey, the data were rescaled and the ratings were converted into percentages.

Importance of Environmental Challenges. The results of both surveys show strong recognition of the importance of environmental challenges (statement 5-1.). In the McKinsey international survey, 92% of the respondents agreed that "the environmental challenge is one of the central issues of the 21st century." Overall, 94% of the Hungarian respondents also agreed that environmental issues will be crucial in the coming century and there was relatively little difference among the responses of executives of companies in different ownership groups, with all of the executives of foreign-owned companies strongly agreeing. Perceptions were similar about respon-

TABLE 5. Differences in Perceptions of Environment
(Percentage of Respondents Who Agreed with the Statement)

Statements (Significance level)	Domestic	Mixed	Foreign	Hungary Total	McKinsey Survey
5-1. The environmental challenge is one of the central issues of the twenty-first century.	94	93	100	94	92
5-2. The industry will have to re-think its entire conception of the industrial process if it is to adapt profitably to an increasingly environment-oriented world.	67	72	50	67	63
5-3. Where environmental or health considerations demand it, the sale of our products will be curtailed or their production halted, regardless of our economic interests. (p = 0.044)	23	24	67	25	NA
5-4. Pollution prevention pays.	56	33	50	54	76
5-5. There is a need to assume responsibility for one's products even after they left the plant.	95	97	100	96	83
5-6. In the long term our spending on environmental R&D will give us a competitive advantage.	65	63	50	64	76
5-7. To minimize the chance of future tragedies, we should pursue a partnership of government, indus-try and academia. (p = 0.110)	83	62	67	79	80

sibility for the environmental impacts of products (statement 5-5 in Table 5).

Need for New Partnerships to Solve Environmental Problems. A strong consensus also existed in both surveys on the need for new partnerships to solve environmental problems and prevent new ones in the future (statement 5-7). About 80% in the international survey and 79% in the Hungarian survey, agreed on the need to pursue partnerships among government, industry, and academia in order to minimize the chance of future tragedies. However, in Hungary this statement was viewed differently–at 11.0% significance level using the Kruskal-Wallis test–among respondents from companies in dif-ferent ownership groups. Executives from the domestic companies, having had long experience with government involvement, agreed the most (83%) about the need for new types of partnerships that include academia and the private sector. The other two groups–62% of those from mixed-ownership companies and 67% from foreign-owned companies–agreed, but somewhat less strongly.

Benefits of Environmental Management. A majority of corporate respondents agreed in both the international and Hungarian samples–although at a somewhat lower level of consensus than existed on broader issues–that actions to manage environmental problems would benefit their companies. However, differences appeared in both the strength of agreement between international and Hungarian executives, and about ways in which environmental actions would benefit companies among managers of different types of companies in Hungary. About 76% of the executives responding to the McKinsey-survey agreed that long-term spending on environmental R&D (statement 5-6) would give their companies a competitive advantage. In Hungary only about 64% of all executives and only about half of those from foreign-owned companies agreed with the statement.

About 76% of international respondents also agreed that pollution prevention pays for companies (statement 5-4). But in Hungary only 54% of the executives thought that pollution prevention would result in benefits for the company, and among those from mixed-ownership companies only one-third agreed. Small differences also appeared when respondents were asked how extensively their companies would have to reorient their practices and procedures. About 63% of the international respondents and 67% of the Hungarian respondents agreed to the statement (5-2) that "industry will have to re-think its entire conception of the industrial process if it is to adapt profitably to an increasingly environment-oriented world." Perhaps because to some degree foreign-owned companies had already adopted more environmentally-friendly manufacturing processes and because they are operating mostly in the less environmentally sensitive industries, only half of the executives in this ownership group agreed.

Perceptions of Appropriate Company Policies and Practices

Given the relatively strong consensus among corporate executives internationally and in Hungary on the critical environmental challenges facing companies in the future, both the McKinsey and the Hungarian surveys sought to clarify how executives perceived these challenges in their own companies and what types of changes they were prepared to support.

Key Environmental Concerns. Some differences appeared in the responses of executives throughout the world who were surveyed by McKinsey, and in those of Hungarian executives from companies in different ownership groups, on the operational implications of their concerns. In the McKinsey survey, "complying with regulations" was the main environmental concern followed by "preventing incidents." Both are typical of traditional "defensive" environmental management approaches. About half as much importance was assigned to the next two (more proactive) concerns, "enhancing positive image" and "integrating environment into corporate strategy." The least important consideration for the international companies was "realizing new market opportunities," while for the companies operating in Hungary it was the key concern. Interestingly, the participants in the Hungarian study and the international survey agreed on the importance of the next two items: "preventing incidents" and "enhancing positive image." "Complying with regulations" and "integrating environment into corporate strategy" were the least important issues for the respondents from Hungary, perhaps because of the uncertain circumstances they had to deal with during the economic transition. Complying with regulations may have seemed less important because Hungary's regulations are strict but not effectively enforced. The economic crisis largely focused Hungarian managers' attention on issues of survival and they may have therefore underestimated the importance of corporate strategy.

Curtailing Environmentally Harmful Products. Although a majority of respondents to both surveys agreed with general statements about the seriousness of environmental challenges and the benefits to companies of taking positive actions to improve environmental management, only 25% of Hungarian respondents agreed that companies should curtail production of or remove products for health or environmental reasons. The results show that statement 5-3 was viewed significantly differently (at 4.4% significance level) by respondents in the three ownership groups. Managers from foreign-owned companies tended to agree more strongly (67%) that if environmental considerations demand it, the sale or manufacture of a product should be halted regardless of the economic interests of the company. Only about 23% and 24%, respectively, of the executives from domestic and mixed-ownership companies agreed with that statement.

Seriousness of Environmental Issues in Value-added Chain. Respondents were asked in the McKinsey study to identify the phase of a product's life cycle where environmental issues were most serious. The international respondents reported production as being the most critical phase; followed by disposal and recycling. Product use and sourcing were at the end of the list. Hungarian executives had somewhat different perceptions. They felt that environmental issues were most serious in disposal and recycling and showed less concern about production, sourcing of raw materials, and product use. This difference can be explained by the fact that Hungary's 1986 hazardous waste law created a large gap between the volume of waste production and the level of waste disposal capacity. There was strong agreement in all ownership categories in Hungary on the need for improving waste management and manufacturing technology and far less agreement on improving end products. A much higher percentage of executives from foreign-owed companies thought that improvements in end products would improve environmental protection than did their counterparts in domestic or mixed-ownership companies.

Most Effective Government Policy Instruments. A question about the most effective government policy instruments for addressing major environmental issues was unique because differences in political culture should influence the attitudes of managers. The McKinsey survey showed that 63% of the Japanese respondents (double the average response) preferred direct regulation, while self-regulation and market mechanisms were strongly favored by North American managers. Direct regulation may be more strongly preferred by managers of companies in countries with stable political situations or with governments having more transparent economic policies. Indirect regulation and self-regulation were mainly favored in stable market economies like the United States. The international and Hungarian surveys also sought to elicit executives' perceptions about the most effective means of achieving environmental protection. The major differences between international and Hungarian respondents appeared to be on the efficacy of direct regulation (e.g., command and control) and positive indirect regulation (e.g., subsidies, tax breaks). Hungarian managers were less disposed toward direct regulation—not because they preferred indirect regulation, which was even more problematic for them—but because Hungarian environmental protection legislation started with the command and control instruments and Hungarian managers may have better understood how unrealistic that approach really was. After 1989 the new government introduced some economic instruments such as fuel taxes, deposits for tires, and ecotaxes on packaging, and it reduced subsidies for public transport and eliminated tax breaks for environmental protection investments. Perhaps this experience led Hungarian managers to prefer positive incentives over indirect regulation through negative incentives (e.g., taxes, pollution charges) and "self-regulation" (e.g., voluntary restraint of production).

About 59% of the respondents in Hungary thought that the current legal regulations greatly contributed to environmental protection. However, this overall response masked large differences among the three ownership groups. The level of agreement ranged from 33% for foreign-owned companies and 58% for Hungarian-owned establishments to 69% for companies with mixed ownership. These differences were significant at the 14.3% level on the Kruskal-Wallis test for the original five-point scale responses. One possible explanation for the joint ventures' high level of satisfaction with current regulations is the number of concessions made by the government in order to attract foreign investment. The desire on the part of the Hungarian government to increase foreign investment in order to improve economic conditions may have temporarily superseded its concern about environmental conditions. Joint venture managers would be reluctant to change the regulations under which they negotiated their arrangements and to curtail production of environmentally damaging products.

Environmental Practices Currently Used. Finally, the greatest differences between international and Hungarian respondents were seen in the types of environmental practices already adopted. Hungarian companies lagged behind in all categories. Significant differences were also seen among Hungarian companies in different ownership groups. For example, while 79% of international companies have written environmental policy statements, only about 57% of domestic Hungarian companies and 67% of foreign-owned Hungarian companies have adopted such policies. About half of the international respondents reported that their companies have a board member with specific responsibility for environmental issues; but in Hungary only 39% of domestic companies, 33% of foreign companies, and 23% of mixed companies had such board members. About 43% of the McKinsey respondents said that their companies had public communications programs on environmental issues, but in Hungary only one-third of the foreign-owned firms, 8% of the domestic firms, and 13% of the mixed-ownership companies have such programs. (See Table 6.) Only a very small percentage of domestic (6.4) and mixed companies (3.3) and none of the foreign companies in Hungary used environmental performance evaluations for their suppliers, while 22% of the executives in the international survey reported that their company followed this practice.

TABLE 6. Environmental Policy Component that is Currently Installed at the Company

Policy Component	Percentage of Companies with the Component			
	Domestic (Hungary)	Mixed (Hungary)	Foreign (Hungary)	McKinsey Survey
1. Written company policy statement.	57	77	67	79
2. Board member with specific responsibility.	39	23	33	52
3. Environmental performance evaluation of suppliers.	6	3	0	22
4. Hiring external experts in environmental affairs.	19	13	17	27
5. Public communication program.	8	13	33	43
6. Environmental marketing program.	26	27	33	32

Although about one third of the companies had some kind of an environmental program in place, the use of these programs differed from market to market among the companies operating in Hungary. In the Hungarian questionnaire several additional questions addressed the issue of environmental marketing. Generally, these questions asked managers what they thought about their customers and the potential for marketing green products. There was no statistically significant difference in any of these questions among the different ownership groups, showing that although the managers disagreed on several environmental issues, they saw their operating environment, the Hungarian market and their Hungarian customers quite similarly. The first question was about the importance of the green nature of a product for customers. Only about 7% of the domestic companies and joint ventures, and about 17% of the foreign companies thought that the green nature of the product is important or very important for their customers. Similarly, only a minority of the respondents thought that their customers would pay 5% more for a "green" product. This agreement was further supported when the managers were asked about the importance of emphasizing the green nature of the products in developed market economies, in other foreign markets, and in the domestic market. The answers showed a clear trend: an overwhelming majority of the respondents thought that it is very important to emphasize the green nature of a product in the developed market economies, somewhat less important in other foreign markets, and not very important in the Hungarian market.

FINDINGS AND CONCLUSIONS

The Hungarian survey showed that there is virtually no difference between the environmental perceptions of Hungarian and international managers of the importance of environmental challenges. If anything, Hungarian executives are slightly more sensitive to the importance of environmental issues and more strongly agree that companies are responsible for the environmental impacts of their products even after they leave the factory. Hungarian executives also strongly agree with their international counterparts on the need for new partnerships of government, business, and academia to address environmental issues, and seem to be less trusting that government or businesses alone can solve environmental problems. Although Hungarian managers agree with their international counterparts that environmental actions will benefit companies, the level of that agreement was much weaker than that of international executives on the statements that their industries would have to entirely rethink their industrial processes and that pollution prevention would result in benefits for their companies.

It was surprising, however, that respondents to the McKinsey survey saw very little distinction between Central and Eastern European and third world countries in terms of the most appropriate approaches to developing clean technologies or the environmental barriers to foreign acquisition of companies. Despite some large economic, political and social differences in the two regions, executives from around the world had virtually the same attitudes toward the appropriate approaches to developing clean technologies in Central and Eastern Europe and third world countries. A little over 40% believed that training local management and staff in clean technologies was the best approach for both regions; about 20% thought that subsidies, soft loans, and tax provisions would promote the adoption of clean technologies; and smaller percentages favored transfer of expatriate experts to operate facilities, development of special "fool-proof" technologies, and access to patents at minimal or no charge. Their perceptions of the barriers to higher foreign investment in Central and Eastern Europe and third world countries were also similar, except on two dimensions: more than twice as many international respondents thought that potential environmental liabilities would be barriers to foreign acquisition of companies, and a far larger percentage thought that the cost of upgrading facilities would be a stronger barrier to foreign investment in Central and Eastern Europe than in third world countries.

When attention was focused on the specifics of how companies should deal with environmental issues, there were some strong differences in perceptions between Hungarian and international respondents and among Hungarian respondents from companies in different ownership groups. Only a minority of Hungarian executives from domestic and mixed-ownership companies, for example, agreed that the production or sale of a product should be halted because of environmental considerations.

Most Hungarian managers saw the most serious environmental implications in disposal and recycling and in production processes, whereas for international respondents disposal and recycling were perceived to be less urgent problems, perhaps because in Western European, Japanese, and American companies these problems were no longer as compelling. More than their international counterparts, Hungarian managers favored indirect regulation and use of incentives as the most effective means of protecting the environment. Generally the managers of joint ventures and domestic companies in Hungary thought that current legal regulations were contributing to environmental protection, while executives of foreign companies did not strongly agree. This disagreement might be attributed in part to the small number of foreign-owned companies in the sample, but it is more likely due to the current economic conditions in Hungary where managers focus more on "marketization" and attracting foreign investment than on strengthening environmental controls.

When asked about environmental actions currently used by their companies, the responses of Hungarian executives showed that their companies lagged behind their international counterparts in all categories of actions. Beyond having adopted environmental policy statements or designated a board member to be concerned with environmental issues, a relatively small percentage of Hungarian companies have adopted other means of meeting environmental challenges. A relatively high percentage of companies reported the existence of environmental marketing programs. However, marketing "green" products or the "green" nature of the products was thought to be much more important in developed market economies than in the Hungarian market.

Although there seems to be a wider gap between Hungarian and Western European and North American companies in adopting more effective environmental practices, the survey revealed that Hungarian managers are acutely aware that their companies will have to invest more heavily to achieve higher levels of environmental protection in the future. As Table 7 indicates, more than 77% of the respondents from domestic companies predicted an increase or a significant increase in environmental protection-related company investments in the future, as did 80% of those from mixed-ownership companies, and 88% from foreign-owned companies. If these predictions are accurate reflections of the plans these executives are making for future investment, it seems to indicate that neither domestic companies nor multinationals anticipate operating in Hungary in a way that can evade or ignore the increasing pressures to address environmental challenges in the future.

Finally, the evidence from these surveys indicates that executives from around the world are highly sensitive to the importance of environmental issues, and that foreign-owned companies in Hungary are not seeking a "pollution haven" in which to manufacture at a lesser standard environmentally than they do in Europe or North America. A recent survey of foreign investors in joint ventures undertaken by the Hungarian Academy of Science's Institute for World Economics for a Japanese aid organization confirms this impression (Csáki, 1993). It concludes that "most companies think about environmental protection as a normal feature [of doing business], a necessary condition of production, and are ready to equip their facilities with up-to-date equipment." Indeed, the study found that the lack of clear and enforceable environmental regulations leaves most multinational companies uncertain about how to make those investments and about their future liability for environmental degradation. American companies were particularly concerned about the impact of weak environmental regulations on their decisions and on their ability to sell products made in Hungary in Western European markets. They generally saw the move toward

TABLE 7. Change of Environmental Protection Related Company Investments in the Immediate Future (Percentage Distribution)

Investment Trend Forecast	Domestic	Mixed	Foreign
Decrease	4.9	6.7	0
Constant	17.1	13.3	16.7
Increase	68.3	70.0	50.0
Significant Increase	9.7	10.0	33.3

more transparent environmental regulations and more effective enforcement in Hungary as a way of improving the business climate.

END NOTES

1. The McKinsey "Corporate Response" questionnaire was distributed to participants of the Annual Meeting of the World Economic Forum (held in Davos in February 1991), the Second World Industry Conference on Environmental Management (WICEM II, organized by the International Chamber of Commerce in Rotterdam, April 1991), and the 19th Annual General Meeting of the International Primary Aluminum Institute (held in Amsterdam in May 1991). Efforts were made to generate responses from specific geographic regions in order to ensure a sufficient response from these areas. The five regions were based on the geographic location and the GNP per capita of the country where the company headquarters were located:

- North America (consisting of Bermuda, Canada, and the United States), Japan, Western Europe (consisting of the European Community and the EFTA countries);

- Central and Eastern Europe (consisting of former centrally planned economies of Bulgaria, Czechoslovakia, Hungary, Poland, Soviet Union and Yugoslavia); and

- Third World (consisting of the developing countries in South America, Africa, and Asia).

Responses from Australia, Hong Kong, New Zealand, Singapore, Taiwan and the United Arab Emirates were included in the overall analysis but they were excluded from any regional segmentation because of lack of sufficient numbers relative to the variety of countries.

The industrial classification of the sample included six groups: (1) chemicals (covering chemicals, rubber, and plastic), (2) energy (including utilities, energy distributors and oil, coal, and gas companies), (3) metals (including primary metals, metal products and machinery), (4) process industries (including paper and paper products, glass, construction and building materials), (5) consumer goods (including food, beverage and tobacco, textiles and apparel, and pharmaceuticals/diagnostics), (6) durables (including transport equipment, electrical machinery/appliances, electronics/telecommunications, aviation, and environmental technology).

In many parts of the questionnaire the respondents were asked how strongly they agreed or disagreed with certain statements or whether an issue was critical or unimportant. The scale used ranged from 1 (disagree or unimportant) to 5 (agree or critical). The ratings were converted into percentages (1 and 2 as disagree, 3 as neutral, 4 and 5 as agree).

2. The overall results of the McKinsey survey may be somewhat optimistic on corporate executives' perceptions of the environmental challenge because: (1) most of the responses were from senior executives who are, generally, more strategically oriented and more optimistic about environmental matters than their lower level, more operational counterparts; (2) about 59% of the respondents were from large, international companies that may have had greater exposure to environmental issues, and therefore were more environmentally sensitive; and (3) respondents who attended the World Industry Conference on Environmental Management, WICEM II, can be expected to be more positive about environmental issues than those who did not attend.

REFERENCES

Cairncross, F. (1992). *Costing the Earth: The Challenges for Governments, the Opportunities for Business*, Cambridge, Mass.: MIT Press.

Csáki, G. (1993). *Foreign Direct Investments and Joint Ventures in Hungary: A Basic Issue of Transformation Towards a Market Economy*. Budapest, Hungary: Hungarian Academy of Sciences, Institute for World Economics.

Daniel, W. W. (1990). *Applied Nonparametric Statistics* (2nd ed.). Boston, Mass.: PWS-Kent.

Frosch, R. & N. Gallopulas (1987). Strategies for Manufacturing. *Scientific American* (September): 144-153.

Hansen, P. (1989). Criteria for Sustainable Development Management of Transnational Corporations. *Industry and Environment*, Vol. 12, Nos. 3-4: 32-42.

Jackson, T., R. Costanza, M. Overcash & W. Rees (1993). The Biophysical Economy–Aspects of the Interaction Between Economy and Environment. in T. Jackson (ed.) *Clean Production Strategies* (pp. 3-28). Boca Raton, Fla.: Lewis Publishers.

Kemp, R. (1993). An Economic Analysis of Cleaner Technology: Theory and Evidence, in K. Fisher & J. Schot (Eds.) *Environmental Strategies for Industry* (pp. 79-113). Washington, D.C.: Island Press.

McKinsey & Company (1991). *The Corporate Response to the Environmental Challenge, Summary Report*. Amsterdam, The Netherlands: McKinsey & Company.

Panayotou, T. (1993). *Green Markets: The Economics of Sustainable Development*. San Francisco, Calif.: ICS Press.

Pearson, C. S. (1987). *Multinational Corporations, Environment and the Third World: Business Matters*. Durham, N.C.: Duke University Press.

Rondinelli, D. A. (Ed.). (1993). *Privatization and Economic Reform in Central Europe: The Changing Business Climate*. Westport, Conn.: Quorum Books.

Rondinelli, D. A. & M. R. Fellenz (1993). Privatization and Private Enterprise Development in Hungary: An Assessment of Market Reform Policies. *Business & The Contemporary World*, 5(4), 75-88.

Schmidheiny, S. and the Business Council on Sustainable Development (1992). *Changing Course: A Global Business Perspective on Development and the Environment.* Cambridge, Mass.: MIT Press.

Schot, J. & K. Fischer (1993). The Greening of the Industrial Firm, in K. Fischer & J. Schot (Eds.), *Environmental Strategies for Industry* (pp. 3-33). Washington, D.C.: Island Press.

United Nations Commission on Transnational Corporations (UNCTC) (1990). *Transnational Corporations and Issues Relating to the Environment.* New York: United Nations.

Vári, A. & P. Tamás (Eds.). (1993). *Environment and Democratic Transition: Policy and Politics in Central and Eastern Europe.* Boston, Mass.: Kleuwer Academic Publishers.

White & Case Inc. (1994). Hungary. in European Bank for Reconstruction and Development, *Investors' Environmental Guidelines* (pp. 223-288). London: Graham & Trotman Publishers.

World Bank (1994). *Social Indicators of Development.* Washington, D.C.: World Bank.

What's in a Label? Environmental Issues in Product Packaging

Debbora A. Whitson
Walter A. Henry

SUMMARY. This exploratory study represents the first attempt to provide empirical data as a part of a growing research stream to support guidelines for environmental labeling practices. Using standard marketing research conjoint analysis practice, four distinct clusters of consumers were found along with relative utilities for various environmental label conditions within each cluster. Recommendations are made for developing guidelines and establishing industry standards. *[Article copies available from The Haworth Document Delivery Service: 1-800-342-9678. E-mail address: getinfo@haworth.com.]*

HISTORICAL EXAMINATION

The issue of environmental awareness or the lack of it has its origins in the Industrial Era immediately following World War II.

Debbora Whitson is Associate Professor of International Business and Marketing at California Polytechnic University, Pomona, 3801 W. Temple Avenue, Pomona, CA 91768. Walter Henry is Full Professor, Graduate School of Management at the University of California, Riverside, A. Gary Anderson Building, Riverside, CA 92521.

The authors wish to thank unknown reviewers for their helpful comments.

[Haworth co-indexing entry note]: "What's in a Label? Environmental Issues in Product Packaging." Whitson, Debbora A. and Walter A. Henry. Co-published simultaneously in *Journal of Euromarketing* (International Business Press, an imprint of The Haworth Press, Inc.) Vol. 5, No. 3, 1996, pp. 29-42; and: *Green Marketing in a Unified Europe* (ed: Alma Mintu-Wimsatt, and Héctor R. Lozada) International Business Press, an imprint of The Haworth Press, Inc., 1996, pp. 29-42. Single or multiple copies of this article are available from The Haworth Document Delivery Service [1-800-342-9678, 9:00 a.m. - 5:00 p.m. (EST). E-mail address: getinfo@haworth.com].

The move of the country was one of plentiful untapped resources. During this time built-in obsolescence was considered good business practice among many. Only a few companies considered environmental issues when developing their marketing strategy. The Amway Corporation, for example, was started in 1959 with minimal packaging and biodegradable and concentrated products. In 1989, Amway was the first corporation in the private sector to receive the United Nations Environmental Achievement Award. Amway's 32-year history of manufacturing environmentally safe products as well as networking other companies' environmentally friendly products prompted its receipt of the U.N. Award (Sharkey, 1990).

There is some evidence that in Europe the "green marketing" trend originated earlier than in the United States. A case in point is the logo and labeling program called Blue Angel which was established in West Germany in 1978. In England massive green efforts began to surface in the early eighties (Redmond, 1988). One example is the success of Body Shop, a retailer whose product mix features natural ingredient cosmetics and biodegradable toiletries.

In response to the green movement the European Commission (EC) has designed guidelines to distinguish products that meet minimum environmental standards (Thayer, 1993). The EC set out to develop criteria for 20 consumer products groups, but so far agreement has been reached on only one category: dishwashers and washing machines. Manufacturers originally supportive of the idea are deserting in droves as disagreements over criteria pit one industry niche against another. Domestically, a number of nonprofit organizations have begun to develop seal of approval programs to standardize the use of environmentally friendly claims. As a first attempt to qualify environmentally friendly claims the Green Cross Certification Corporation launched the nation's first environment seal of approval program (Freeman, 1990). Companies receiving the Green Cross had to specify on their labeling the amount of recycled material that their product contains. According to Linda Brown, VP-Communications for Green Cross, the certification does not attest to the environment friendliness of a product; it only gives reference to the amount of recycled material contained in the product. Consumers' interpretation of this distinction is vital to the success of the Green Cross Certification Program.

The Green Seal Inc., formally known as the Alliance for Social Responsibility, announced its plans to introduce a seal that would label environmentally friendly products by soliciting advice from manufacturers, public interest groups, trade associations and government officials (Fisher, 1990, June 18). Although the rationale for selecting the five product categories initially pinpointed for this approval program (i.e., light bulbs, laundry cleaners, house paints, toilet paper and facial tissues) was not explained, it was noted that in determining the criteria for light bulbs, Green Seal could look at whether the package material and the bulbs themselves are recyclable. Once approved, marketers could use the seal in advertising and labeling for three years. The empirical exploratory research described in this paper looked at possible criteria for laundry cleaners which was one of the product categories initially included in the Green Seal's approval program.

Norman Dean, the program's executive director, estimated that the first seal was to be awarded early in 1991. However, the sealing program has yet to be implemented. Category criteria and participation costs are currently being operationalised.

Many marketers are opting not to participate in any private third-party endorsement programs. Procter & Gamble, Kimberly-Clark Corporation, and Colgate-Palmolive, to name a few, are choosing to cautiously wait until governmental guidelines are established for green claims (Fisher, 1990, April 23). Once the government provides a consensus on what the criteria should be for biodegradable, green, recycled and environmentally friendly products, seal approving programs will be more readily accepted (Hindle, White & Minion, 1993). The use of seals along with other "green" strategies provides an excellent opportunity to gain market share (Scerbinski, 1991; Ottman, 1993; Fitzgerald, 1993). Davis (1992) and Stern (1991) caution companies against putting on the environmentalist mask without long-term investments in the planning and development of green products.

In addition to the preceding historical look at the subject, a review of the literature was conducted to examine the research findings.

LITERATURE REVIEW

Estimates show that there are 15 million environmentally concerned households in the United States today, and by 1995 the number is projected to more than triple to 52 million (Klein, 1990). A 1988 *New York Times*/CBS news poll found that 80% of the participants felt that environmental protection is of vital importance no matter what the cost (Jay, 1990). In another survey over 30% of the respondents indicated that they were extremely interested in purchasing environmentally safer packaging and less than 3% expressed no interest (*Good Housekeeping* Reader Poll, 1989). When asked if they would be willing to pay a little more for this packaging a majority (77%) responded yes.

The issue of how much more consumers are willing to pay for environmentally sound products has been examined in Britain. According to a Mintel poll, 27% of Britons said they would pay a premium of 20% or more for green goods (*Economist*, 1989). Domestically, however, a recent report by Gerstman & Meyers Inc., New York, said consumers would pay only 5% more for a product as long as it offers what they want (Miller, 1990). A survey of packaging executives found that a number of companies are taking the wait-and-see attitude when it comes to alerting their packaging design (Teague/Gallup poll, 1990). Fifty-eight percent of the respondents felt that consumers would accept price increases, 28% felt they would not and 14% did not know. A majority (51%) said they have not altered their packaging to make it environmentally friendly and 47% had. This data suggests that manufacturers are interested in incorporating green into their packaging, but they do not want to spend the money because they are afraid that consumers will not support the resulting higher prices. In line with these findings a series of Roper Reports surveys (between 1990 and 1992) have shown the number of consumers willing to pay a premium of at least a "moderate" amount extra for lower polluting cars, gasoline, and detergents has fallen from an average of 43% to only 32% across six categories (Bradford, 1992).

Perhaps one of the largest consumer surveys (N = 5,000) performed indicated that 80% of the respondents strongly agreed that they would like to see a lot less packaging, less plastic and more recycling (Graham, 1990). Another survey done in July 1990, showed that out of 600 people randomly phoned (Freeman & Dagnoli, 1990), 25% have stopped buying products from at least one company because they believed the company was not a good environmental citizen (e.g., Exxon). The Council on Economic Priorities (CEP), which publishes a shopper's guide with environmental performance ratings of 168 companies, found that 70% of their subscribers have switched brands based on the ratings in the book and 64% said they referred to the book whenever they shopped.

In a special issue of *Advertising Age* (Chase, 1991) the results of a Gallup Survey (N = 1,514) reports that P & G, a firm who has exhibited environmental concerns in its products and packaging, received the top ratings, being named by six percent of the respondents as the most environmentally conscious company. McDonald's, another firm who has made strategic changes in its packaging based on concerns of consumers for environmental friendliness, came in second place with four percent of the total, but 66% of those surveyed said "none" or "don't know." Thirty-four percent indicated that the Green Seal had a great impact on their purchase decisions. Other tested categories received the following percentages: "No Phosphate" detergent label (26%), Federal governmental guidelines (25%), "Concentrated" laundry detergent (21%), recycled plastic bottle label (19%) and recycled bottle TV ad (16%).

In one of the few systematic examinations of environmental advertising claims, Carlson (1993) found that claims which exalt the environmental benefits of products (e.g., "This product is biodegradable") were more often classified as misleading and deceptive. Claims that were designed to enhance the environmental image of an organization (e.g., "We are committed to preserving our forests") were more prone to be labeled as vague/ambiguous. The more acceptable claims were those containing environmental facts (e.g., "The world's rain forests are being destroyed at the rate of two acres per second"). Such practices can lead to confusing or misleading product claims which are not advisable within the legal environment facing businesses today.

There is a substantial amount of interest in implementing "green" in the marketing mix, however, empirical research on this topic has been provisional (Miller, 1993). The purpose of the present exploratory study is twofold: first and foremost to provide additional empirical data as a part of a growing research stream to support guidelines for implementing "green" into the marketing strategy, and secondly to systematically begin the investigation of consumers' perception of seals of approval and other labeling practices.

EXPLORATORY RESEARCH METHODOLOGY

Selection of Product Category and Stimulus Factors

Laundry detergent was selected because it is a basic household product in which some manufacturers have shown environmental interest. Using standard marketing research conjoint analysis procedure, samples of leading brands were examined to determine the relevant labeling stimuli along with their respective levels (Green & Wind, 1975). Observations yielded the following: package size (regular versus compacted–aka, concentrated), chemical descriptions (phosphates vs. phosphate-free), Suds Factor (no mention vs. low suds), and price (low–$4.39 vs. high–$6.99). The two price points selected represented the average high and low detergent prices for an 18-load package found in grocery stores in the Los Angeles area at the time of data collection. The two seals of approval, the Green Seal and Green Cross at two levels (present vs. not) were also included as labeling stimuli. A convenience sample of 125 laundry detergent buyers took part in the research. The respondents were selected to provide a wide range of both males and females and ages from 18-56 years old, residing in southern California. A standardized orthogonal design was used to construct sixteen package labeling conditions (Green & Rao, 1971). Table 1 illustrates the labeling conditions used for the sixteen hypothetical detergents.

Respondents were given sixteen labeling conditions cards (one card for each hypothetical detergent) and were told that each card represents a brand. Respondents were requested to rank each card from the one they would most likely buy to the one they would least likely buy. To make the task easier they were told to sort their cards

TABLE 1. Standardized Orthogonial Design Table

Card	Price	Box Size	Suds	Phos.	Green Seal	Green Cross
1	0	0	1	1	0	0
2	0	0	1	1	1	1
3	0	0	0	1	0	1
4	0	0	0	1	1	0
5	1	0	1	0	0	0
6	1	0	1	0	1	1
7	1	0	0	0	0	1
8	1	0	0	0	1	0
9	0	1	1	0	0	0
10	0	1	1	0	1	1
11	0	1	0	0	0	1
12	0	1	0	0	1	0
13	1	1	1	1	0	0
14	1	1	1	1	1	1
15	1	1	0	1	0	1
16	1	1	0	1	1	0

Price: 0 = Low; 1 = High
Box Size: 0 = Regular; 1 = Concentrated
Suds: 0 = With Suds; 1 = Low Suds
Phosphates: 0 = Phosphates; 1 = No Phosphates
Green Seal: 0 = No Green Seal; 1 = Green Seal
Green Cross: 0 = No Green Cross; 1 = Green Cross

into three piles–one for those they may buy, one for those they probably would not, and the middle stack for undecided. Each stack was ranked within and the three stacks were then merged with the most liked on top and least liked on the bottom. Finally respondents were asked to mark the entire stack in ascending order (one through 16).

A dummy variable regression analysis was conducted for each respondent. Each hypothetical detergent provided a single observation with the recorded preference ranking being the dependent variable and the six label conditions becoming the independent variables. Each respondent's regression run consisted of 16 observations and the "zeros" and "ones" of Table 1 become the appropriate level for each independent variable. The regression beta coefficients (parts worths) associated with each labeling condition therefore represent a relative utility measure for each condition for the respective respondent.

A cluster analysis was conducted to search for groupings of respondents with common label condition utility profiles. In essence what we searched for were groups of respondents who shared similar feelings about the importance of price, package size, phosphate level, sudsing, and the display of the Green Seal or the Green Cross emblems.

RESULTS

Four distinct clusters were observed accounting for 89% of the convenience sample used in the study. The 11% of the respondents were scattered and did not fall into any distinct grouping. The four distinct clusters were named as follows; Price Sensitive (46% of sample), Package Convenience (11%), Environmentally Concerned (22%), and Symbolic Environmentally Concerned (10%). Figure 1 illustrated the relative utility (i.e., value to the respondent) for each label condition for each cluster. The utilities illustrated on Figure 1 are the average part worths that were estimated from the dummy variable regression analysis discussed above. The reader is cautioned that the respondents were from a convenience sample and the percentages given above do not necessarily represent the distribution of the groups in the actual population.

Figure 2 illustrates the relative importance of each label condition for each group on a common scale. This allows the clusters to be more readily compared. For the Price Sensitive respondents price equates to 53% of the total utility range observed for the group. Detergent price is by far the most important labeling condition for these respondents. Conversely, for the Package Convenience group the fact that the product is concentrated accounts for 46% of the total utility range and was their predominant decision variable. The remaining two clusters show almost equal relative importance of approximately 26% for the display of either the Green Seal or the Green Cross. The larger of the two groups also rates the importance of phosphate-free at 32% while the environmental group labeled Symbolic Environmental Concern rates the importance of the variable at only 9%. For the convenience sample observed, 32% of the respondents appeared as though some form of environmental seal of approval would be a major part of their decision.

If the price-utility relationship exhibited by the respondents can be assumed to provide an average dollar metric for utility for each of the groups, a rough approximation could be found for the worth to the respondent of the Green Seal and the Green Cross being displayed on the package. Carrying out these calculations revealed that the estimated dollar value of the utility gained in a displayed seal for the Price Sensitive and the Package Convenience group was on average $0.84. Conversely, the estimated dollar value of a seal for the environmentally concerned portion of the sample was $6.14.

When demographic information was used to attempt to predict group membership, no significant relationships were observed.

CONCLUSION

This study represents an exploratory attempt to examine the implications of greenness in products and in labeling practices. Although there appears to be considerable confusion on the part of consumers and manufacturers about the meaning of the terminology of greenness, there does seem to be some early evidence that a portion of consumers do place some value on the environmental responsibility of manufacturers. The convenience sample was large enough to support the findings for the sample itself, however, further research needs to be conducted with a generalizable sample to determine the extent of the present findings in the general population.

The introduction of two different sealing programs (i.e., Green Seal and Green Cross), calls for additional research. This research should specifically examine consumer interpretations of the "green" symbols. Do consumers understand the differences between these symbols? If not, should efforts be made to teach the differences or should a universal symbol be used? Another important issue to be considered is whether a seal approving program should be housed in a governmental agency or a nonprofit organization.

The outcome of this research suggests that environmental awareness under some circumstances (i.e., laundry detergent in southern California) may be a factor that should be incorporated into the

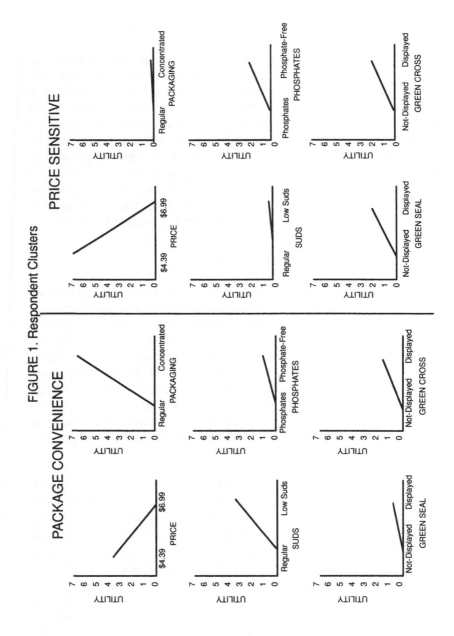

FIGURE 1. Respondent Clusters

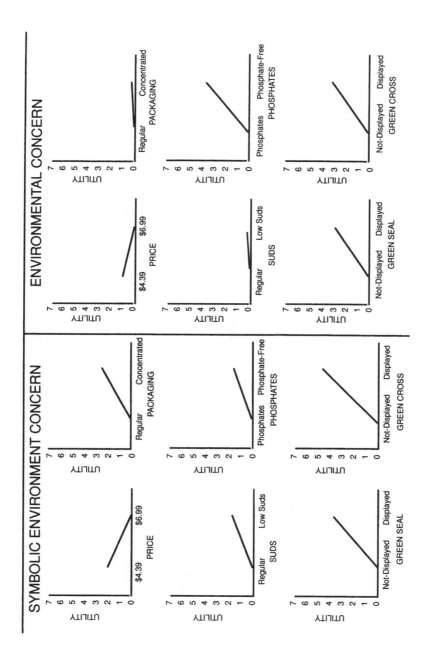

FIGURE 2. Label Condition Relative Importance

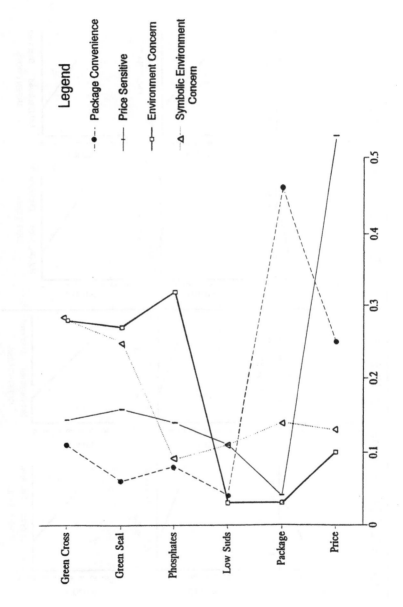

40

strategic marketing plan. However, the issue of how to effectively implement green packaging within stringent economic times is vital and warrants further investigation. The good news is that this may represent a golden opportunity for marketers who choose to effectively master the production and promotion of environmentally safer products and/or packaging.

REFERENCES

Bradford, Fay (1992), "The Environment's Second Wave," *Marketing Research: A Magazine of Management & Applications* (December), 44-45.

Carlson, Les; Grove, Stephen; Kangon, Norma (1993), "A Content Analysis of Environmental Advertising: A Matrix Method Approach," *Journal of Advertising* (September) 27-39.

Chase, Denies (1991), "Ad Age Gallup Survey," *Advertising Age* (January 29), 8-10.

Davis, Joel (1992), "Ethics and Environmental Marketing," *Journal of Business Ethics* (February), 81-87.

Economist (1989), "The Perils of Greening Business," (October 14), 75-76.

Fisher, Christy (1990), "'Green Seal' Programs Flowering," *Advertising Age* (April 23), 76.

_____(1990), "Green Seal Unveils Plan," *Advertising Age* (June 18), 1, 88.

Fitzgerald, Kate (1993), "It's Green, It's Friendly, It's Wal-Mart," "Eco-Store," *Advertising Age* (June 7), 1, 44.

Freeman, Laurie (1990), "Eco-Approval, First Marketers Get Green Cross," *Advertising Age* (September 3), 54.

_____ and Dagnoli, Judan (1990), "Green Concerns Influence Buying," *Advertising Age* (July 30), 10.

Good Housekeeping Institute Report (1989), "Convenience Foods & the Microwave," (April), Consumer Research Department.

Graham, Judith (1990), "Dows Ads Boost Plastics," *Advertising Age* (January 29), 26.

Green, Paul and Rao Vithala (1971), "Conjoint Measurement for Quantifying Judgmental Data," *Journal of Marketing Research*, Vol VIII (August), 355-363.

_____and Wind, Yoram (1975), "New Way to Measurement Consumers' Judgments," *Harvard Business Review* (July-August), 107-114.

Hindle, Peter; White, Peter; Minion, Kate (1993), "Achieving Real Environmental Improvements Using Value: Impact Assessment," *Long Range Planning* (June), 36-48.

Jay, Leslie (1990), "Green About the Till: Markets Discover the Eco-Consumer," *Management Review* (June), 24-28.

Klein, Easy (1990), "The Selling of the Green," *D&B Reports*, v38n5 (Sept/Oct), 30-31, 35.

Miller, Cyndee (1990), "Use of Environment-Friendly Packaging May Take Awhile," *Marketing News* (March 19), 18.

_____(1993), "Conflicting Studies Still Have Executives Wondering," *Marketing News* (June 7), 1, 12.

Ottman, Jacquelyn (1993), *Green Marketing: Challenges & Opportunities for the New Marketing Age*, McGraw-Hill Inc., New York.

Redmond, Steve (1988), "Greens Roll On After Ozone Win," *Marketing* (UK) (July 28), 15.

Scerbinski, Jacqueline (1991), "Consumers and the Environment: A Focus on Five Products," *The Journal of Business Strategy* (September/October) 44-47.

Schlossberg, Howard (1990), "'Greening' of America Awaits Green Light from Leaders, Consumers," *Marketing News* (March 19), 1, 16.

Sharkey, Betsy (1990), "Will Green Marketers Get Red Light?," *AdWeek* (March 12), 32.

Stern, Alissa (1991), "The Case of the Environmental Impasse," *Harvard Business Review*, (May/June), 14-29.

Thayer, James (1993), "EC's Green Audit Makes Manufacturers See Red," *Journal of European Business* (Nov/Dec), 62.

Forty Shades of Green:
A Classification of Green Consumerism
in Northern Ireland

A. J. Titterington
C. A. Davies
A. C. Cochrane

SUMMARY. This paper examines the various classifications of green consumerism that have been compiled in the United Kingdom and elsewhere. By means of a series of longitudinal studies the breadth and depth of commitment of the green consumer is identified. The Northern Ireland consumer exhibits similar environmental concerns to other consumers in the United Kingdom. Based on these studies an overall classification of green consumerism in Northern Ireland is compiled. *[Article copies available from The Haworth Document Delivery Service: 1-800-342-9678. E-mail address: getinfo@haworth. com.]*

BACKGROUND

During the eighties, pressure groups such as Greenpeace and Friends of the Earth drew the public's attention to the major environ-

A. J. Titterington, C. A. Davies, and A. C. Cochrane are affliated with Information Management Division, School of Finance and Information, The Queen's University of Belfast, Belfast BT7 1NN, Northern Ireland.

[Haworth co-indexing entry note]: "Forty Shades of Green: A Classification of Green Consumerism in Northern Ireland." Titterington, A.J., C.A. Davies, and A.C. Cochrane. Co-published simultaneously in *Journal of Euromarketing* (International Business Press, an imprint of The Haworth Press, Inc.) Vol. 5, No. 3, 1996, pp. 43-63; and: *Green Marketing in a Unified Europe* (ed: Alma Mintu-Wimsatt, and Héctor R. Lozada) International Business Press, an imprint of The Haworth Press, Inc., 1996, pp. 43-63. Single or multiple copies of this article are available from The Haworth Document Delivery Service [1-800-342-9678, 9:00 a.m. - 5:00 p.m. (EST). E-mail address: getinfo@haworth.com.].

43

mental problems confronting the earth. National governments and in-
ter-governmental bodies also expressed concern about issues such as
pollution, acid rain, the ozone layer and the conservation of rainforests.

A poll conducted in sixteen countries by the CNN/Angus Reid
group in 1992 (see Figure I) found that there was widespread public
concern about environmental issues in all of these countries. In fact
a poll average of 86% of respondents taken across all the countries
either 'moderately agreed' (32%) or 'strongly agreed' (54%) with
the statement 'I am very worried about the state of the environment'. The response in Britain was 26% and 60%, respectively.

Manufacturers of a wide range of products have voluntarily, or in
response to legislation, made an effort to play their part in tackling
environmental issues. Initially there was a great burst of enthusiasm
on the part of manufacturers, retailers and consumers to develop a
green stance. It is beginning to be recognised by all that the issue is
no longer if they are green, but the extent of their greenness (Mitchell and Levy 1989). As a former president of the Institute of Chartered Accountants indicated, 'Companies setting the pace on environmental issues will be seen as the leaders of the corporate sector'
(Macve and Carey 1992).

FIGURE I

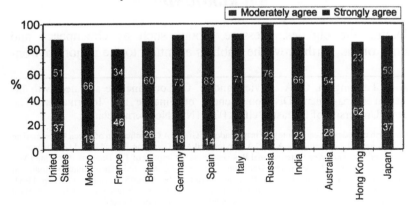

I am very worried about the state of the environment

Source: CNN/ Angus Reid Group World Poll 1992

Developments in manufacturing technology have resulted in more environmentally friendly products. Cars can run on lead-free petrol and have catalytic converters to reduce pollution. The producers of washing powders and detergents have attempted to modify their products to have less environmental impact and the manufacturers of leading brands such as Persil and Ariel now promote their green credentials in advertising campaigns and on their packaging. Paper products such as stationery and lavatory paper, etc., are produced with greater respect for the environment. An area which has received much publicity is the reduction in the use of chlorofluorocarbon (CFC) gases in the manufacture of aerosols and in refrigeration, air-conditioning and foam-blowing.

Clearly, many manufacturers have responded positively to the green agenda, although it is debatable whether this is out of genuine concern, to comply with environmental legislation, or out of a need to maintain market share in an increasingly competitive atmosphere by reacting to green consumer behaviour. Marketers saw opportunities for launching new products and gaining competitive advantage and an increasing range of products was marketed as environmentally friendly.

A 1991 study by Marketing Intelligence Services Ltd. estimated that there had been a highly significant increase in the number of new green products launched in the United States in the period 1985-1991. The designation of a new greener product inevitably includes both those products which have been revised to be more environmentally friendly and those which, in Ottman's terms, 'sport green claims' (Ottman 1992). There were 810 new greener products launched in 1991 compared to just 24 in 1985. However, what is probably more important was that greener products formed a higher percentage of all new product launches for this period. These accounted for 13.4% of all new products launched in 1991 as opposed to just 0.5% of new products in 1985 (see Figure II). The findings of another study by Market Intelligence Services in 1992 which looked at the importance of green products in a range of countries would appear to indicate that similar patterns of greener new product launches are emerging throughout the world.

The green consumer assumed such importance in marketing that some manufacturers jumped blindly onto a green bandwagon. Ad-

FIGURE II

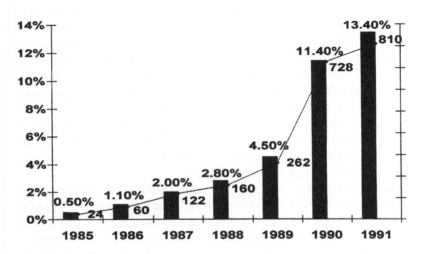

vertising agencies and research bodies (Hoggan 1989; Kreitzman 1989) conducted surveys which indicated that consumers would buy environmentally friendly products and might even be prepared to pay more for them. In response to these research findings manufacturers sought to incorporate 'greener' imagery and environmental claims in their advertising campaigns with a fourfold increase in the number of environmentally themed or oriented print and television advertisements between 1989 and 1991.

However, as the public grew more educated in green matters, they became aware of the superficial nature of the environmental friendliness of some products. Friends of the Earth initiated the 'Green con of the year' in 1989 for the organisation which had done the most to hoodwink the public (Plachta 1989). Award winners included Fisons for an advertisement which made spurious claims about their peat-cutting operations and ICI in relation to the extent of their commitment to the Montreal protocol for the phasing out of ozone-depleting chemicals.

With an increasing range of environmentally friendlier products on the market, retailers have taken the green challenge on board. Many of the large United Kingdom multiples such as Gateway,

Tesco and Sainsburys have devoted significant shelf space to environmentally friendly products. Gateway won the green marketing award in recognition of its efforts to promote products with a reduced environmental impact. The publication of the *Green Consumer's Guide* (Elkington and Hailes 1988) followed by the *Green Consumer's Supermarket Shopping Guide* (Elkington and Hailes 1989) further raised public awareness and the number of legal actions invoked by the latter were indicative of its impact (Elkington 1991).

Concern for health issues has increased. In the United Kingdom, government reports into the extent of heart disease brought about healthy eating programmes (Darral 1991). Hanssen's best-selling *E for Additives* (1986) drew the public's attention to the variety of products routinely included in foodstuffs some of which were later linked with behavioural problems in children. Various personalities became associated with campaigns to reduce the amount of pesticides used, especially Apple Alar. The great 'Egg Debate' about the level of salmonella in eggs caused the resignation of a British Cabinet Minister. Significant damage was done to the British meat industry by BSE or mad cow disease. Similarly, there was a high level of public concern about the use of hormones (BHT) to increase milk yield in cattle. All of these health scares have had an influence on the increasing number of consumers opting for healthier, more environmentally friendly organic foods.

The throw-away eighties may be characterised as the apogee of consumerism, while the caring eco-sensitive nineties are now in vogue. The limited nature of the earth's resources was epitomised in water shortages in various areas of southeast England. The rise of the eco-thriller as a genre on British television is indicative of the effect on popular consciousness. Instead of lip service to green issues, more fundamental concerns are the order of the day. In response to demand from companies, the British Standards Institute published BS7750, the world's first standard for environmental management systems (Economist 1991). However, green issues may be counterbalanced by the global recession; where consumers may have the profundity of their attitudes tested by financial imperatives, some may ask if they can afford to be green.

A PROFILE OF THE GREEN CONSUMER

As Croydon (1992) emphasises, green consumers are 'not a marginalised minority'. The level of interest is reflected in the mass of market research on environmental-related issues published in the United Kingdom and elsewhere. This has led to various classifications of green consumers being suggested including those by Diagnostic Social and Market Research 1990 (see Figure III) and in the United States by the Roper Organisation in 1992. However, the most relevant profile of the typical green consumer can be drawn from a review of the latest findings (McKenzie 1991; Mintel 1991 a b c d e; Mintel 1992).

Women are more concerned than men about environmental issues, as 71% mentioned at least one issue, compared with 61% of men. Those with children are more likely to boycott a product because of an environmental issue, again with the ozone layer top of list. Three quarters of ABs could think of at least one environmental issue that would stop them buying a product or service (Mintel 1991a b).

FIGURE III

BEING SEEN TO BE GREEN–

A Classification of Green Consumerism

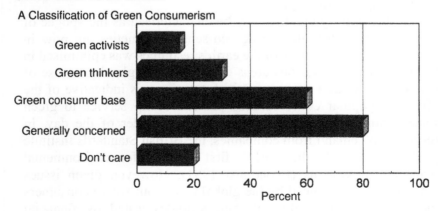

Source: Diagnostics Social and Market Research, 1990

These findings indicate three major characteristics attributed to the green consumer; they are likely to be female, with children and in the social grouping classifications ABC1.

Based on surveys carried out in England, Scotland and Wales, Mintel classifies consumers by their willingness to buy environmentally friendly products (EFPs) into dark, light and armchair greens (see Figure IV). The dark greens—people who claim to seek out green goods actively—comprise 39% of the sample. They are more likely to be female, with children, influenced more by quality than price and use the green grapevine or personal recommendations when making purchasing decisions.

Some 20% are pale greens, buying such goods only when they see them; divided evenly between the sexes, they tend to be in the age groups 25-34 and 55-64. They are more price sensitive in their buying habits than their darker green counterparts.

Nearly one quarter of respondents are armchair greens, who care about the environment but have not changed their purchasing habits accordingly. Here men are in the majority, and consumers are definitely price led. Only 1 in 10 are not concerned at all about the

FIGURE IV

Mintel Classification of Green Consumerism

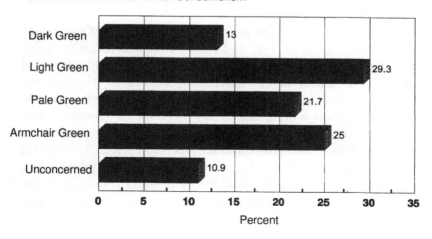

environment, with 2% positively anti-green, making an effort to avoid green products.

It is worth noting that confusion and ignorance do not appear to have much influence on the inclination to buy green products; those who seek out EFPs are just as confused about the claims as other respondents and those who do not buy them are only slightly more likely than others to be sceptical about the prices charged.

Apart from teenagers, who have limited purchasing power, Mintel concludes that the consumers most committed to the environment tend to be female, aged between 35 and 44, from ABC1 socio-economic groups, and shop at supermarkets with the fullest shopping trolleys as they have older and hungrier children. Knowledge of the green consumer is important particularly for the retail industries as environmental issues affect the spending habits of nearly six in ten respondents, in that they buy or try to buy environmentally friendly products.

The bases of these and similar classifications are criticised by Bohlen, Schlegelmilch and Diamantopoulos (1993) because of a lack of rigour in segmentation on the basis of environmental concern. They attempt to develop indicators of greenness based on (1) perceived knowledge about green issues, (2) attitudes towards environmental protection and (3) levels of environmentally sensitive purchasing, recycling and other environment-related behaviour. It is interesting to assess how these results compare with the work carried out in Northern Ireland.

The current paper is based primarily on the results of two major surveys carried out in 1991-92 and 1993-94 but also refers to earlier studies carried out by the authors. The 1991-92 study attempted specifically to assess actual purchasing behaviour (through the products they purchase) and consumers' commitment to environmentalism (by their willingness to pay more for EF products). Initially it was considered more important to attempt to construct a meaningful classification of consumer greenness primarily based on actual behaviour, which could prove of immediate use to manufacturers in helping them understand the changes in consumer behaviour due to environmentalism, rather than attempt a more complex model.

The focus of the 1992-3 study addressed many of the concerns expressed by Bohlen et al. in that it covers not only purchasing and other EF behaviours, and willingness to pay more for EF products, but also knowledge about environmental issues including environmental labelling; attitudes towards environmental protection; and membership of environmental pressure groups. The results of this study should enable greater refinement of the current classification in line with Bohlen's criticism of existing classifications.

NORTHERN IRELAND SURVEYS

These findings are based on a series of longitudinal studies carried out in Northern Ireland over the period 1989-93. The objectives of these studies were to quantify the extent of green activities among consumers in the four major areas–organic food (OF), lead free petrol (LFP), environmentally friendly cleaning agents (EFC) and recycling (REC). In so doing a classification has been established for the extent and level of commitment of green consumer behaviour.

Study 1. 1989-90 study of 200 urban and rural motorists interviewed about their usage of lead free petrol.

Study 2. 1989-90 study of 150 shoppers looking at purchasing of organic food and environmentally friendly cleaning products.

Study 3. 1989-90 study of 200 urban households investigating their recycling activity.

Study 4. 1991-92 Omnibus study of 1033 urban and rural consumers investigating their purchasing behaviour/activity in respect to organic food, lead free petrol, environmentally friendly cleaning products and recycling.

Study 5. 1992-93 Omnibus study of 1003 urban and rural consumers investigating their purchasing behaviour/activity in respect to organic food, lead free petrol, environmentally friendly

cleaning products and recycling; their membership in environmental organisations; their knowledge and understanding of the
major environmental problems and how individual purchasing
behaviour could influence these problems; and their opinions
about current and proposed environmental labelling schemes.

Studies 1-3 were of the nature of preliminary studies in this area
and the samples taken are simple convenience samples. Some
attempt was made, however, to ensure that a minimal degree of
bias was included, i.e., there was a spread of sampling locations
and the proportion of male to female respondents was in line with
the demographic profile of Northern Ireland. For the two omnibus
surveys, the population of Northern Ireland was stratified by
county and the sample weighted according to the population numbers in each county. Respondents were interviewed in the major
market town or towns of each county. This was based on the
assumption that these respondents would be representative of residents of the county. The sample was selected by random route
sampling. The accuracy of the results based on the samples for the
omnibus surveys has been calculated to be of the order of ± 3% at
the 96% confidence level. The findings concerning each of the key
areas are now examined in turn, comparing the results with existing research in Great Britain.

Use of Lead Free Petrol (LFP)

This area has shown significant changes with the passing of time
(see Table 1). It is currently the most popular of the green activities
measured, with half the sample participating.

Those interviewed gave their main reason for using lead free
petrol as being environmental concern (58%) and cost saving
(38%). Their main reasons for not using lead free petrol were the
cost of conversion of the engine (53.4%) and reduced efficiency/
performance (33.3%).

The most important factors considered when buying fuel were
price (49.2%), performance (34.7%) and environment (16.1%). The
major reasons, apart from using diesel, for not using lead free petrol
were that their car was not capable (63.4%), the performance of the

TABLE 1: Usage of Lead-Free Petrol

Usage of lead-free petrol	Study 1 1989-90	Study 4 1991-92
Use lead-free petrol	20.5%	49.7%
Use leaded petrol	65.5	41.4
Diesel	14	8.9
$\chi^2_2 = 18.77$ which is significant at the 0.5% level		

car suffers (13.4%) or damage to engine (9%). Just under half (42%) said that they would still use lead free petrol even if it cost more.

These results would indicate a rapid growth in the use of lead free petrol and a higher usage than the overall average in the United Kingdom (33%), but in line with other areas, such as Scotland (36.7%) (Mintel 1991c). This can be attributed to newer cars in Northern Ireland, with stricter roadworthiness testing and various media campaigns by leading fuel companies on local radio. The growth could also be attributed to the phasing out of all leaded fuel except the very expensive (with a significant price differential), the fact that all new cars can take lead free petrol and the removal of worries about engine damage or loss of performance.

Recycling

Study 3 indicated that 44% of respondents from urban households are involved in recycling (REC) (19% indicating that they did so on a regular basis). Aluminum cans were the most popular area (28%), followed closely by paper (24%) and glass (21%). By 1992, the survey of both urban and rural areas gave 42.2% involvement in recycling. The emphasis had changed, glass (23%) having become the most popular area, followed by cans (18%) and finally paper (14.6%).

The major reasons for not becoming involved in recycling are that it is too awkward, or that people are not interested (49.8%), unaware of collection facilities (45%), with a few indicating that they were unaware of the need to recycle (5.1%). However, the proportion of those who make the effort to take items to collection points is high (see Table 2).

When it comes to paying more for products in recycled packaging, 41% of respondents expressed their willingness to pay more, while 49.4% are unwilling, and 8.8% of respondents neutral.

There would appear, therefore, to be a major and unselfish commitment to recycling by those already involved. This could be further enhanced by the increased advertising of facilities.

Organic Foods

In Study 2, 10% of respondents regularly bought organic foods (OF); two years later, Study 4 reveals that almost 35% of those surveyed are regular buyers. The main reasons for purchasing in Study 2 were health reasons (47%), environmental reasons (28%), and taste (22%). In Study 4 the main reasons were that organic foods were healthier (72.7%), had no additives or sprays (49.9%), taste (35.1%), freshness (33.7%), and environmental reasons (32.9%). The reasons for not buying organic foods are availability and cost (see Table 3).

Respondents to Study 4 indicated they might switch to organic foods if they were more available (34.2%) and cheaper (30.8%);

TABLE 2. Involvement in Recycling

	Paper %	Glass %	Cans %
Take to collection points	68.5	94.8	91.5
Collected from home	30.5	5.2	8.5

TABLE 3. Reasons for Not Buying Organic Food

	Study 2	Study 4
Availability	27%	55.8%
Cost	34	37.1
χ^2_1 = 3.89 which is significant at the 0.5% level		

some, of course, would not switch (18.6%). Cost is obviously a major factor; almost 30% of respondents indicated that they would be willing to pay up to 30% more for organic products. In addition, 39.9% of the sample said that people should pay more for organic foods to protect the environment.

It must be acknowledged that there are extra-environmental factors in the areas of food, with particular emphasis on health issues. The primary reasons for the purchase of organic foods are more likely to be personal interests rather than concern for the general environment, understandably, due to the numerous health scares concerning intensive food production. Nevertheless, concern for the environment remains an important purchasing consideration.

Environmentally Friendly Cleaning Products (EFC)

A high degree of unanimity was apparent in Study 2 with the main reason for purchasing EFC being environmental concern (83%). Study 4 evinced a greater spread of reasons (see Table 4).

Prohibiting factors in Study 2 were given as excessive price and lack of efficiency. In Study 4 these were unavailability (37.3%) and preference for other brands (20.1%); just over half of respondents thought that people should not be prepared to pay more for environmentally friendly cleaning products. Some 35% of those surveyed regularly bought environmentally friendly cleaning agents.

In this area the level of environmental concern has dropped; this may be due to the perceived efficiency of the products and greater efforts being made by leading industry players.

Of the four areas examined, the use of lead free petrol is the most popular (49.7%), followed by recycling (42%). The remaining two,

TABLE 4. Reasons for Purchasing Environmentally Friendly Cleaning Products

Personal concern for environment	54.4%
Concern through advertising	31.4%
General advertising	16.9%
$\chi^2_3 = 5.88$ which is not quite significant at the 0.1% level	

organic food and environmentally friendly cleaning products, tie for third place (35%). Involvement in any of the four areas shows a level of environmental consciousness, although consumers may have additional reasons as well for using lead free petrol and organic food (because of price differential and health benefits). There are few other direct benefits to the consumer in recycling and environmentally friendly cleaning products. A current study is being conducted to determine consumer behaviour and motivation for buying green products, to separate selfish motives from real 'greens'.

WHO ARE THE GREEN CONSUMERS?

These studies demonstrate a certain consistency with previous market research in that whilst differences in Tables 5, 6,7 and 8 do not test significantly for χ^2 at the 0.05% level, they do indicate to some degree that women are more likely to be green consumers (see Table 5); women are more likely to pay extra (see Table 6); the presence of children is likely to be significant with a somewhat greater distinction between the purchasing patterns of these households and those without children (see Table 7).

The primary importance of the socioeconomic grouping is in relation to the amount of personal disposable income (see Table 8).

There would appear to be some correlation between spending power and environmental issues. Whether it is negative, i.e., those on low incomes cannot afford to be green, or positive, those with more money are willing to spend on environmentally friendly products, remains to be discussed.

So far both Mintel and the Northern Ireland surveys are in broad agreement. When the age factor is examined, differences appear.

TABLE 5. Green Activity by Gender

	OF%	EFC%	LFP%	REC%
Male	25.9	30.3	31.6	36.1
Female	38.3	36.6	51.0	45.6

TABLE 6. Willingness to Pay More by Gender and by Product Area

		Male %	Female %
OF	Would pay more	35.3	42.4
	Would not pay more	30.6	51.8
EFC	Would pay more	36.4	33.0
	Would not pay more	50.4	52.7
LFP	Would pay more	27.0	37.8
	Would not pay more	62.7	49.0
REC	Would pay more	36.4	43.6
	Would not pay more	51.8	52.1

χ^2_3 is not significant at the 0.1% level

TABLE 7. Green Activity and the Presence of Children

	OF%	EFC%	LFP%	REC%
Children <18	39.4	35.4	51.6	43.7
Others	31.5	31	48.5	41.0

χ^2_3 is not significant at the 0.5% level

According to Mintel, age is an important factor in the profile of the green consumer and their findings indicated that the greenest age groups tended to be the late teens and the 35-44 age group. It would appear from the Northern Ireland surveys that while younger people may well be more interested in environmental issues and pay greater lip service to green purchasing, they will only purchase them if they can afford them. It is mainly those younger people in the groupings with higher disposable incomes who actually translate their environmental concerns into the purchase of green products.

However, many of these young people, while not currently among the dark green/supergreen purchasers of environmentally friendly products, have an important role as influences on their

TABLE 8. Green Activity and Disposable Income

	OF%	EFC%	LFP%	REC%
Income				
< £10K	27.8	30.5	45.6	37.5
10-20	36.2	36.1	44.1	43.5
20-30	40	38.8	56.4	51.4
30-40	36.5	35.4	57.1	40.0
>40	42.2	33.3	51.1	33.3
χ^2_2 is not significant at the 0.05% level				

parents' purchasing patterns and as committed green purchasers of the future.

The fundamental distinction between the two types of survey should be stressed—the Northern Ireland research has primarily concentrated on actual consumer behaviour rather than intentions or willingness and hence may give more accurate determinants of behaviour. It therefore provides a more realistic profile of consumer commitment to environmental matters. Based on these indicators, an accurate picture of the various market segments, or shades of green, can be devised.

SHADES OF GREEN

A classification of greenness can be achieved by assimilating both breadth (number of activities concerned) and depth of commitment (support for the proposition that people should be prepared to pay more for environmentally friendly products). In terms of breadth of activity, the samples for Studies 4 and 5 had the composition as outlined in Table 9 and demonstrate a significant shift in the breadth of green activity.

Depth of commitment is illustrated by agreement to pay more (see Table 10).

Comparing the results of Studies 4 and 5, it can be seen that there has been a significant shift for more environmentally friendly prod-

TABLE 9. Extent of Involvement in Green Activities

	Study 4 1991-1992	Study 5 1992-1993
involved in 4 areas OF, LFP, EFC, REC	4.9%	10.2
involved in 3 areas	12.8	25.8
involved in 2 areas	26.5	26.8
involved in 1 area	31.6	20.3
involved in no areas	24.2	17.0

χ^2_4 = 11.42 which is significant at the 0.05% level

TABLE 10. Willingness to Pay More by Number of Areas

Willing to pay more	Study 4 1991-1992	Study 5 1992-1993
In all 4 areas	5.8	19.6
In 3 areas	21.5	16.4
In 2 areas	20.9	20.3
In 1 area	31.7	20.0
In no area	20.1	23.8

χ^2_4 = 10.35 which is significant at the 0.05% level

ucts. It would appear that the commitment of Northern Ireland consumers to 'greener behaviour' is not only widespread but growing. When breadth is cross-tabulated with depth of commitment (willingness to pay more for green products), it gives the following results. (See Table 11; also Figures V and VI).

As can be seen from the shift in 'greenness' between studies 4 and 5 and from research findings in the United Kingdom and the United States, there is still considerable room for growth in these market segments. However, with some two thirds of the population actively sympathetic towards environmentally friendly products and some 80-90% of the population at least passively worried about the environment, it is obvious that Northern Ireland manufacturers cannot afford to ignore the significant shift in consumer behaviour.

TABLE 11. Northern Ireland and Mintel Classifications

N.I. 1991-92	N.I. 1992-93	Mintel
7.4%	16.7% committed/super green	13.0% dark green
18.7%	23.7% emerging green	29.3% light green
36.6%	26.3% experimental green	21.7% pale green
30.4%	26.1% potential green	25.0% armchair green
7.0%	7.3% anti-green	10.9% unconcerned

FIGURE V. Pie Charts Representing Proportions of Green Consumers Categorised by Commitment.

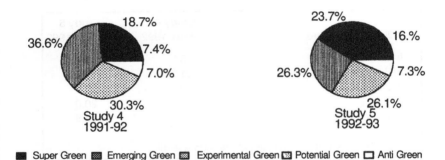

■ Super Green ▨ Emerging Green ▨ Experimental Green ▨ Potential Green ☐ Anti Green

CONCLUSIONS

There appears to be a deep-seated and growing commitment of consumers to either purchase green products or get involved in green activities. Greener consumers appear to be deeply concerned about environmental issues (although they may not fully understand the direct linkages between environmental impact and product purchase or indeed have any real depth of knowledge about specific environmental issues) (Cope and Windward 1991). However, their unease about environmental problems is real enough to make them modify their purchasing patterns/lifestyles to a significant degree. There are some personal benefits from green purchasing behaviour,

FIGURE VI. Breadth of Commitment (Involvement in Green Activities) Cross-tabulated with Depth of Commitment (Agreement to Pay More for EFPs)

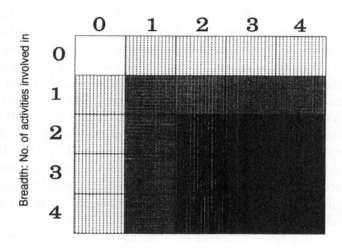

Depth: Think that consumers should be prepared
to pay more for EFPs

		1992	1993
☐	Anti-Green	7.0	7.3
▦	Potential Green	30.4	26.1
▦	Experimental Green	36.6	26.3
▰	Emerging Green	18.7	23.7
■	Super Green	7.4	16.7

but these more selfish motives seem to be outweighed by the more selfless determination of green consumers to "do their bit for the environment" in that they may be prepared to incur inconvenience and pay more for poorer performance products.

This presents both opportunities and threats for individual manufacturers. As green consumers become more sophisticated in terms of linking their purchasing behaviour to real environmental issues, manufacturers who simply try to jump on the green bandwagon by making misleading or erroneous claims will find that it becomes increasingly counterproductive. Equally, those manufacturers who choose to ignore green concerns and continue to market their products solely on the conventional basis of factors such as increased style, performance and value for money, will find that by not addressing an increasingly mainstream purchasing determinant, they will lose market share to greener products. This could be true, even though those greener products may be inferior in terms of conventional marketing advantages and benefits.

Conversely, this new consumer movement offers great potential for those who produce more genuinely environmentally sympathetic products. They can now target increasingly sophisticated green segments of the market which will not only be committed to purchasing greener products but also be prepared to pay more for these products and demand more accurate 'green' advertising of them; as Watts (1992) indicates, eco-labelling may make this obligatory. However, this does not mean that manufacturers can exploit a gullible green market with products which are of grossly inferior performance and for inflated prices. The evidence is there to show manufacturers that while green consumers may be prepared to accept marginally poorer performance products and marginally more expensive products, there are limits to their acceptance.

With 80-90% of consumers at least interested or involved in some sort of green purchasing and some 30-40% quite actively, manufacturers would be extremely foolish to ignore the real opportunities for differentiating products on a green basis and should recognise the potential threats to their products by not addressing a major determinant of future international consumer demand.

REFERENCES

Bohlen, G, Schlegelmilch, BB and Diamantopoulos, A. 1993. Measuring Ecological concern: a multi-construct perspective. *Journal of marketing management 9,* pp. 415-30

Cope, D and Winward, J. 1991. "Information failures in green consumerism." *Consumer policy review* 1 (2) 83-86

Croydon, D. 1992. "Below the line: are green offers dead and buried?" *Marketing* 26 March

Darral, J. 1992. "Health/healthy food: is there a difference?" *Br. food journal* 94 (6) 17-21

Economist. 1992. "Do it our way: a standard for green managers." *The Economist* 16 May

Elkington, J and Hailes, J. 1988. *The green consumer's guide.* London: Gollancz

Elkington, J & Hailes, J. 1989. *The green consumer's supermarket shopping guide.* London: Gollancz

Elkington, J. 1991. "The impact of green consumerism on business." *Consumer policy review* 1 (2) 76-82

Hanssen M. 1986. *E for additives supermarket shopping guide.* Wellingborough: Thorsons

Hoggan, K. 1989. "Shoppers go for green." *Marketing* 16 November 5

Kreitzman, L. 1989. "Green with guilt." *Marketing* 23 February 43-46

Macve, R and Carey, A. 1992. *Business, accountancy and the environment.* London: Institute of chartered accountants in England and Wales

McKenzie, D. 1991. "The rise of the green consumer." *Consumer policy review* 1 (2) 68-75

Mintel. 1991a. *The green consumer.* London: Mintel

Mintel. 1991b. *The green and ethical shopper.* London: Mintel

Mintel. 1991c. "Petrol and oil." *Market Intelligence* September

Mintel. 1991d. "Organic food." *Market Intelligence* January

Mintel. 1991e. "Clothes and dishwashing detergents." *Market Intelligence* March

Mintel. 1992. "Health food shops." *Market Intelligence* September

Mitchell, A and Levy, L. 1989. "Green about green marketing." *Marketing* 14 September 28-35

Ottman, J A. 1992. *Green marketing.* Lincolnwood NTC

Plachta, J. 1989. "Green screens." *Marketing* 30 November 39-42

Watts, N. 1992. "The eco-labelling regulation." *EIU European Trends* 2 68-74

Sustainable Development and International Business: A Holistic Perspective

Héctor R. Lozada
Alma Mintu-Wimsatt

SUMMARY. In this paper, the authors explore the oftentimes controversial philosophy of sustainable development. The potential implications of this philosophy for marketing practitioners are examined. Specific focus is placed on the pioneering efforts of the European Union and on multinational companies doing business in Europe. *[Article copies available from The Haworth Document Delivery Service: 1-800-342-9678. E-mail address: getinfo@haworth.com.]*

Héctor R. Lozada is Assistant Professor of Marketing, School of Management at Binghamton University (SUNY). Dr. Lozada's research interests include marketing theory, marketing strategy and product planning, and green marketing. He has published in a number of professional journals including the *Journal of Consumer Research, Marketing Education Review,* and the *Journal of Organizational Change Management.* Alma Mintu-Wimsatt is Assistant Professor, Department of Marketing & Management at East Texas State University. Her research interests include international negotiations and green marketing. She has published in many professional journals including *Management Science, Marketing Education Review, Journal of Global Marketing,* and the *Journal of International Consumer Marketing.*

This article is made possible in part by the Nuala McGann Drescher Award of the United University Professions (SUNY).

Address correspondence to: Professor Héctor R. Lozada, School of Management, Binghamton University, Binghamton, NY 13902-6000. E-mail: Hlozada@aol.com.

[Haworth co-indexing entry note]: "Sustainable Development and International Business: A Holistic Perspective." Lozada, Héctor R., and Alma Mintu-Wimsatt. Co-published simultaneously in *Journal of Euromarketing* (International Business Press, an imprint of The Haworth Press, Inc.) Vol. 5, No. 3, 1996, pp. 65-74; and: *Green Marketing in a Unified Europe* (ed: Alma Mintu-Wimsatt, and Héctor R. Lozada) International Business Press, an imprint of The Haworth Press, Inc., 1996, pp. 65-74. Single or multiple copies of this article are available from The Haworth Document Delivery Service [1-800-342-9678, 9:00 a.m. - 5:00 p.m. (EST). E-mail address: getinfo@haworth.com].

The preservation, protection, and conservation of the natural environment have become critical areas for most businesses. Since commercial activity entails the utilization of natural resources, sometimes wastefully and inefficiently, many environmentalists have cast business in the role of villain on the environmental scene (Fritsch, Schmidheiny, & Seifritz, 1994). Pressure from various stakeholders—government, special interest groups, consumers—is placed on these businesses, which in turn keeps them under constant and unrelenting watch in their daily operations. Given the legal and regulatory restrictions that they face, the actions of interest groups concerned with the natural environment, and the apparent heightened eco-awareness of consumers worldwide (Bendz, 1993), businesses have the option to remain passive-reactive or to become more proactive in their responses. More proactive businesses have integrated some form of environmentalism into their strategic decision-making process. Particularly interesting is the fact that, controversial as it may be, the philosophy of sustainable development is the environmentalism of choice of some business and government institutions alike.

THE PHILOSOPHY OF SUSTAINABLE DEVELOPMENT

The Ideology

The present-day environmental movement has been largely affected by the philosophy of *sustainable development*. Sustainable development, a concept originally popularized by the 1987 report titled *Our Common Future,* proposes that future prosperity depends on preserving "natural capital"—air, water, and other ecological treasures. This future prosperity requires balancing human activity with nature's ability to renew and rejuvenate itself.

In other words, this idea refers to development that meets the needs of the present without compromising the ability of future generations to meet their own needs (World Commission on Environment and Development, 1987). Two concepts are key:

1. The concept of *"needs,"* particularly the essential needs of the world's poor, which command the utmost priority; and

2. The idea of limitations imposed by the state of technology and social organization on the environment's ability to meet present and future needs (World Commission on Environment and Development, 1987: 43).

The goals of economic and social development must, therefore, be defined in terms of environmental sustainability in all countries. That is, development is taken to mean a progressive transformation of economy and society which is sustainable in a physical or natural environment sense. For example, the notion of physical sustainability cannot be secured unless development policies pay attention to such considerations as changes in access to resources and in the distribution of costs and benefits (World Commission on Environment and Development, 1987).

Its Application to International Business

While the ideas on sustainable development are not the only methods for "greening" international business activities, we believe that embedded in the World Commission's report is a basic ecological approach critical to the preservation, protection, and conservation of our physical or natural environment. That is, concern with a system in which all things are interconnected (Gray, 1990; Kemp & Wall, 1990). This ecological approach does not focus solely on the biological systems, but rather on how the ecosystem interacts with human, social, technical, and economic systems (Gray, 1992; Lovelock, 1982, 1988).

Therefore, from an ecological focus, sustainability would require that societies meet human needs both by increasing productive potential and by ensuring equitable opportunities for all. Additionally, consumption standards everywhere would have to be reassessed so that regard for long-term sustainability, that is, living within the world's ecological means, is safeguarded. As such, it is in this context that we examine some of the basic tasks associated with sustainable development and how they impact international business and, specifically, multinational companies.

IMPLICATIONS: A HOLISTIC PERSPECTIVE

Role of Multinational Companies in the Green Movement

The United Nations Centre on Transnational Corporations (UNCTC) reports that the activities of multinational companies (MNCs) "affect at least one quarter of the world's productive assets, 70 percent of the products in international trade, 80 percent of the world's land cultivated for export crops, and the major share of the world's technological innovations" (UNCTC, 1989: i). MNCs tend also to dominate environmentally sensitive sectors including minerals, oil (petrol) and gas development, agribusiness, and chemicals. Because of all of these factors, worldwide attention has been placed on MNC operations and their activities related to the preservation, conservation, and protection of our physical or natural environment (Rappaport & Flaherty, 1992).

International business organizations, MNCs in particular, are finding it is necessary to conscientiously include environmental management in their list of top strategic priorities. If for any other reason, since the mid to late 1980s (and somewhat as a result of tragedies such as Union Carbide's Bhopal MIC gas leak) businesses face an increased number of environment, health, and safety policies. Consequently, there is rapid proliferation of *environmental development programs* in most MNCs' agendas (Coddington, 1993; Schmidheiny, 1992). Yet, managers should be aware that implementing such programs would entail not only a revision of current policies and procedures, but may also require some restructuring.

Frause and Colehour (1994) warn that some of the problems with the implementation of environment-related policies may arise due to the fact that most managers trained in business schools or on the job prior to the 1990s have not received any formal preparation on how to study and/or deal with the relationships between the natural environment and business. Thus, one of the top priorities would be to make changes in the current corporate culture that would facilitate the formation of environmental programs. In this regard, Kleiner (1990) asserts that people who try to radically change corporations from within are often stymied. "Corporate culture and political pressures provide almost insurmountable resistance against any sudden and even enlightened change" (Frause & Colehour, 1994: 110). An assessment of corporate commitment becomes essential in this light.

The fact that our physical or natural environment is now being acknowledged as a limited resource is forcing MNCs to act as *citizens of the world*. The accelerated manner in which Mother Earth is being destroyed is causing businesses, governments, and the public (i.e., society) to consider the ramifications of their actions–how the actions of, and interaction between, these three sectors *ought not* to be a cause of environmental problems, but rather, a help in the identification of creative solutions. That is, in order to effectively understand environmental problems and provide solutions, a symbiotic relationship or partnership has to exist between the triad members. The successful implementation of a philosophy of sustainability would require not only a reassessment of business policies and practices, but also clarifications and simplifications of government rules and regulations, and changes in consumer activities.

It can be expected that much attention will be focused on MNCs' environmental priorities such as toxic waste disposal, recycling, and pollution. As such, MNCs and their subsidiaries need to recognize that concern over the physical or natural environment is neither trivial nor inconsequential. In fact, the potential repercussions necessitate some form of mandate–a corporate rethinking–for businesses to be internally and externally accountable for their role in environmental degradation. External accountability deals with the potential ecological impact of the products MNCs create, manufacture, and market. Internal accountability deals with the operational and production activities of MNCs that could have some adverse consequences on the preservation, conservation, and protection of the natural environment.

It is also misleading to believe that environmentalism and economic growth are two conflicting business objectives. That is, that an inverse relationship exists between these two objectives. Multinational corporations such as McDonald's, Wal-Mart, and Procter & Gamble acknowledge that the natural environment must be protected and enhanced for economic growth to take place. Accordingly, these companies have taken actions towards that goal (Lodge & Rayport, 1991). McDonald's has made a $100 million commitment to its consumers for recycling purposes. Wal-Mart encourages the purchase of environmentally friendly products and reports that the green labeling programs that they have initiated in 1989 have contributed to an overall 25 percent increase in sales for the year. Procter & Gamble has pledged to spend $20 million per year to develop a composting structure for recycling purposes.

Governments

The European Union (EU), still viewed by some as having the most comprehensive legislative policy on the environment, has recently shifted gears. In December 1992, the EU adopted the European Commission's 5th Environmental Action Programme, which appears to focus less on legislation and more on economic development (Hull, 1994). This attempt by the EU suggests that the relationship between humans, organizations, and the natural environment is being redefined, and the implications thereof are being reinterpreted. At the center of the 5th Programme is the philosophy of sustainable development, forwarding, as a result, performance goals for sustainability rather than legal requirements (Hull, 1994). That is, the 5th Action Programme attempts to enact the European Commission's objective of working voluntarily with industry to attain waste management targets. In contrast to the action programs of the past, the 5th Programme:

1. focuses on the agents and activities that deplete natural resources and damage the environment, rather than waiting for the problems to emerge;
2. aims to initiate changes in behavior through partnership and shared responsibility involving all the relevant sectors of society: public administration, public or private enterprise, and the general public; and
3. broadens the range of instruments applied to any particular problem, that is, moving beyond legislation to market-based instruments, financial support mechanisms, and information, education, and training (cf., Hull, 1994).

The General Advisory Forum on the Environment and Sustainable Development, a consultative body established within the framework of the 5th Action Programme, held its first meeting in January 1994 (Kirschner, 1994). On the agenda were specific directives for the further encouragement of reduction of polluting car emissions, and recovery and recycling targets for the proposed packaging waste directive, which seems to have stemmed from the German program on waste reduction.

The German experience on waste reduction is an interesting case study. The German government enacted a law in 1993 that requires manufacturers to take back the packaging of their products and recycle it. Klaus Topfer, Environmental Minister, has boldly stated that handling waste cannot continue to be the task of the state (ABC News, 1993). In spite of initial reluctance and resistance from manufacturers, the program was implemented. As a result, German retailers and manufacturers have banded together to create a *dual collection system* by which privately funded trucks go through neighborhoods collecting packaging left in special containers. According to the German government, even though the costs are passed along to consumers in the form of slightly increased prices, the average consumer pays less than $3 a month. Manufacturers are now expecting the German government will either (1) enact new laws that will require them to take back their products from consumers and recycle them, or (2) provide new guidelines in accordance with the 5th Programme for voluntary compliance with their waste management initiative. All goods, including cars, television sets and computers, will be targeted. In anticipation, IBM Germany now has a program that dismantles old computers, separates circuit boards, wiring and precious metals, recycles what they can, and sells the rest. Other European countries, such as Austria, Italy, and Great Britain, are looking into the German dual collection system as a model and the guidelines that the 5th Programme provides for their own initiatives.

In summary, we submit that all governments worldwide as well as their respective agencies have to adopt consistent national regulatory policies to provide businesses some environmental guidance and direction. The EU's 5th Action Programme represents a move in that direction. Even when businesses and society engage in behavior that fosters recycling and reusing, a major concern facing governments is waste reduction.

The Public (Society)

In turn, society must not remain apathetic to the solutions that both governments and businesses offer to resolve environmental dilemmas. Goodland, Daly, and Kellenberg (1994) assert that unbridled consumerism in developed nations, marked by increased use of environmental resources, competes with escalating population growth in developing nations as principal threats to sustainability. Moreover, Clark (1994) suggests that we reorient our focus as to enhance the behavioral adjustments that are needed to bring people back to sustainability. We submit that the "throw-away" mentality will be perpetuated unless society stops subsidizing the generation and disposal of garbage. This means changes in current consumers' behavior. To encourage these changes, consumers would have to be provided with information that educates them regarding the relationships among people. Cernea (1993) also suggests that people be provided with a set of values that regulate their behavior with each other and with natural resources. Information and education are pivotal instruments for prompting coordinated social action, inhibiting misbehavior or detrimental behavior, and in developing social capital (Cernea, 1993; Clark, 1994). Hopefully, the ultimate result would be that consumers will favor those products that are friendly to the environment not only as they are consumed, but through their production and later disposal.

Philosophically, the importance of the local or grass roots level also comes into focus. Sustainable development requires the internalization of necessary trade-offs to meet basic needs while protecting the environment and empowering the poor. Realizing that the society is the primary beneficiary of any attempts at sustainable development, individuals will have to readjust their consumption and realign the satisfaction of needs with the more environmentally friendly options that industries would offer. Governments in turn must keep the pressure to comply with environmental standards that society at large can set as appropriate for a better quality of life.

CONCLUSION

While the policy of sustainability may be intuitively appealing, it is inevitable that its implementation will be faced with strong resistance. In particular, three critical areas of possible resistance are recognized.

First, from a macro level, many developing and less-developed countries will find it hard to comply with the tenets of sustainable development. When countries are plagued with meeting the *basic survival needs* of its citizens–concern for the natural environment may be secondary. Second, medium and small-scale companies will have to forego short-term gains for long-term benefits. That is, some initial investment outlay may be necessary to institute environmentally-friendly business activities. Third, from a micro level, some managers believe that the green movement is simply the 1990s version of a "hot" bandwagon. As such, this does not necessitate any drastic adaptation of environment-related policies such as sustainable development.

In order to overcome the aforementioned potential sources of resistance, the collaboration or alliances between businesses, governments, and societies may be necessary. Indeed, these efforts may even have to transcend national borders–to form alliances with other countries plagued with the same ecological problems. The EU's 5th Action Programme seems to be a move in this direction. Collaborative efforts are necessary not only to reduce costs and risks of pioneering and implementing environmental initiatives but also to benefit from the sharing of technology and scientific knowledge. After all, ecological dilemmas were, in part, created by businesses, government and societies.

Perhaps, MIT's Peter Senge summarizes the plight of sustainable development best:

> We're basically living off our capital and compromising the future well-being of generations to come. It's ironic that business is the most likely institution [to master change], but it has the greatest capacity to reinvent itself. (*Chief Executive,* March, 1995, p. 62)

REFERENCES

ABC News (1993, March 10). World News Tonight with Peter Jennings. *Capital Cities-ABC.*

Bendz, D. J. (1993). Green Products for Green Profits. *IEEE Spectrum*, 30(9), 63-66.

Cernea, M. M. (1993). The Sociologist's Approach to Sustainable Development. *Finance & Development*, 30(4), 11-13.

Chief Executive (1995, March). The Pied Piper of Learning, 62.

Clark, M. E. (1994). Integrating Human Needs into Our Vision of Sustainability. *Futures*, 26(2), 180-184.

Coddington, Walter (1993). *Environmental Marketing.* New York: McGraw-Hill.

Consumer Reports (1991, October). Selling Green, 687-692.

Frause, B. & Colehour, J. (1994). *The Environmental Marketing Imperative.* Chicago: Probus Publishing.

Fritsch, B., Schmidheiny, S., & Seifritz, W. (1994). *Towards an Ecologically Sustainable Growth Society.* Berlin: Springer-Verlag.

Goodland, R., Daly, H., & Kellenberg, J. (1994). Burden Sharing in the Transition to Environmental Sustainability. *Futures*, 26(2), 146-155.

Gray, R. (1990). *The Greening of Accountancy: The Profession After Pearce.* London: Chartered Association of Certified Accountants.

_____(1992). Accounting and Environmentalism: An Exploration of the Challenge of Gently Accounting for Accountability, Transparency, and Sustainability. *Accounting, Organizations and Society*, 17 (5), 399-425.

Hull, R. (1994). Reaching for Sustainable Development. *Across the Board*, 31(4), 50.

Kemp, P. & Wall, D. (1990). *A Green Manifesto for the 1990s.* London: Penguin.

Kirschner, E. (1994). Sustainable Development Gets into Gear. *Chemical Week*, 154 (Jan. 26), 20.

Kleiner, A. (1991, July-August). What Does It Mean to be Green? *Harvard Business Review*, 4-11.

Lodge, G. & Rayport, J. (1991, September-October). Knee-Deep and Rising: America's Recycling Crisis. *Harvard Business Review*, 128-139.

Lovelock, J. (1982). *Gaia: A New Look at Life on Earth.* Oxford: Oxford University Press.

_____(1988). *The Ages of Gaia.* Oxford: Oxford University Press.

Magraw, D. (1994). NAFTA's Repercussions: Is Green Trade Possible? *Environment*, 36 (2): 14-20, 39-45.

Rappaport, A. & Flaherty, M. F. (1992). *Corporate Responses to Environmental Challenges.* New York: Quorum Books.

Schmidheiny, S. (1992). *Changing Course: A Global Business Perspective on Development and the Environment.* Cambridge, MA: The MIT Press.

United Nations Centre on Transnational Corporations [UNCTC] (December 18-20, 1989). Criteria for Sustainable Development Management of Transnational Corporations. Background paper No. 1, Expert Group meeting.

World Commission on Environment and Development (1987). *Our Common Future.* Oxford: Oxford University Press.

Index

Note: Page numbers followed by f indicate figures; page numbers followed by t indicate tables.

Advertising Age, 33
Age, as factor in green consumerism, 56-57
Alliance for Social Responsibility, 31
Amway Corporation, environmental awareness of, 30
Apple Alar, 47
Ariel, 45
Australia, environmental concerns of, 44f

Blue Angel, 30
Body Shop, 30
Bohlen, G., 50
Brown, L., 30-31
BS7750, 47

Carlson, L., 33
Catalytic converters, 45
Cernea, M.M., 72
Chlorofluorocarbon (CFC) gases, reduced usage of, 45
Clark, M.E., 72
Cochrane, A.C., 3
Colehour, J., 68-69
Colgate-Palmolive, in green claims, 31
Converters, catalytic, 45
Corporate executives, perceptions on environmental issues, Hungarian companies *versus* international companies, 5-27

Council on Economic Priorities (CEP), 33
Croydon, D., 48

Daly, H., 72
Davies, C.A., 3
Davis, J., 31
Dean, N., 31
Diagnostic Social and Market Research, 48, 48f
Diamantopoulos, A., 50
Dual collection system, 71

E for Additives, 47
Economic conditions, in Hungary, 8-10
'Egg Debate', 47
Elkington, J., 47
Environmental awareness, Green Seal in, 31
guidelines for products, 30-31
historical examination of, 29-31
in households, prevalence of, 32
literature review, 32-34
of Amway Corporation, 30
Environmental development programs, 68
Environmental issues, challenges related to, in Hungarian and international companies, 14-15,15t
concern about, men *versus* women, 48

For Product Safety Concerns and Information please contact our EU
representative GPSR@taylorandfrancis.com Taylor & Francis Verlag GmbH,
Kaufingerstraße 24, 80331 München, Germany

Printed and bound by CPI Group (UK) Ltd, Croydon, CR0 4YY
08/05/2025
01864338-0001